Authors:
Fiona Macdonald studied history at Cambridge University, England, and at the University of East Anglia. She has taught in schools, adult education and universities, and is the author of numerous books for children on historical topics.

Jacqueline Morley studied English at Oxford University. She has taught English and History, and now works as a freelance writer. She has written historical fiction and non-fiction for children.

Artists:
David Antram was born in Brighton, England, in 1958. He studied at Eastbourne College of Art and then worked in advertising for fifteen years before becoming a full-time artist. He has illustrated many children's non-fiction books.

Mark Bergin was born in Hastings, England, in 1961. He studied at Eastbourne College of Art and has specialised in historical reconstructions, aviation and maritime subjects since 1983. He lives in Bexhill-on-Sea with his wife and three children.

Series creator:
David Salariya was born in Dundee, Scotland. He has illustrated a wide range of books and has created and designed many new series for publishers in the UK and overseas. David established The Salariya Book Company in 1989. He lives in Brighton, England, with his wife, illustrator Shirley Willis, and their son Jonathan.

Editors: **Stephen Haynes**
Karen Barker Smith

Editorial Assistant: **Mark Williams**

PAPER FROM SUSTAINABLE FORESTS

Published in Great Britain in MMXI by
Book House, an imprint of
The Salariya Book Company Ltd
25 Marlborough Place, Brighton BN1 1UB
www.salariya.com
www.book-house.co.uk

ISBN-13: 978-1-907184-83-3

S A L A R I Y A

1 3 5 7 9 8 6 4 2

A CIP catalogue record for this book is available from the British Library.

Printed and bound in China.

Visit our website at **www.book-house.co.uk** or go to **www.salariya.com** for **free** electronic versions of:
You Wouldn't Want to be an Egyptian Mummy!
You Wouldn't Want to be a Roman Gladiator!
You Wouldn't Want to be a Polar Explorer!
You Wouldn't Want to sail on a 19th-Century Whaling Ship!

Previous editions © MMIII, MMIV, MMV, MMVIII, MMX

Avoid fighting in the First Crusade! (MMV) (FMacD, MB)
HB ISBN-13: 978-1-905087-49-7
PB ISBN-13: 978-1-905087-50-1

Avoid being in a Medieval Castle! (MMVIII) (JM, DA)
HB ISBN-13: 978-1-906370-25-1
PB ISBN-13: 978-1-906370-26-8

Avoid working on a Medieval Cathedral! (MMX) (FMacD, DA)
HB ISBN-13: 978-1-906714-25-3
PB ISBN-13: 978-1-906714-26-0

Avoid being a Medieval Knight! (MMIV) (FMacD, DA)
HB ISBN-13: 978-1-904642-07-7
PB ISBN-13: 978-1-904642-08-4

Avoid being in a Medieval Dungeon! (MMIII) (FMacD, DA)
HB ISBN-13: 978-1-904194-53-8
PB ISBN-13: 978-1-904194-54-5

You wouldn't want to live in the Middle Ages!

Written by
Fiona Macdonald
Jacqueline Morley

Illustrated by
David Antram
Mark Bergin

Created and designed by
David Salariya

The Danger Zone™

BOOK HOUSE

Contents

The Middle Ages

'The Middle Ages' is the name we give to one of the most exciting periods in European history, from about AD 1000 to around 1500. This was the age of knights in shining armour and damsels in distress. Don't you wish you'd lived at such a romantic time?

Think again!

Life for ordinary people in the Middle Ages could be pretty grim. Most were peasants – poor farmers who worked on their lord's land and had no hope of doing anything else. If you lived in a town, you might be carried off by the plague, or caught up in a cruel siege. Few people lived to a ripe old age. Being a monk or a nun might sound like an easy option, but theirs was a life of hard work and constant prayer.

And suppose you were lucky enough to be born into a noble family and become a knight or a lady? Knights had to be ready to put on their heavy, sweaty armour and fight at a moment's notice. They might be expected to go on Crusade in the Middle East, not knowing whether they would ever return home. And if their castle was attacked while they were away, it would be their lady's job to defend it.

And yet...

This was also the age that gave us mighty castles and glorious cathedrals, many of which are still standing today. It gave us magnificent art and stirring poetry, such as the stories of King Arthur and his knights.

Though their lives were hard, and often short, medieval people achieved great things.

So, what kind of life might you have had in the Middle Ages?

Avoid fighting in the First Crusade!

Introduction

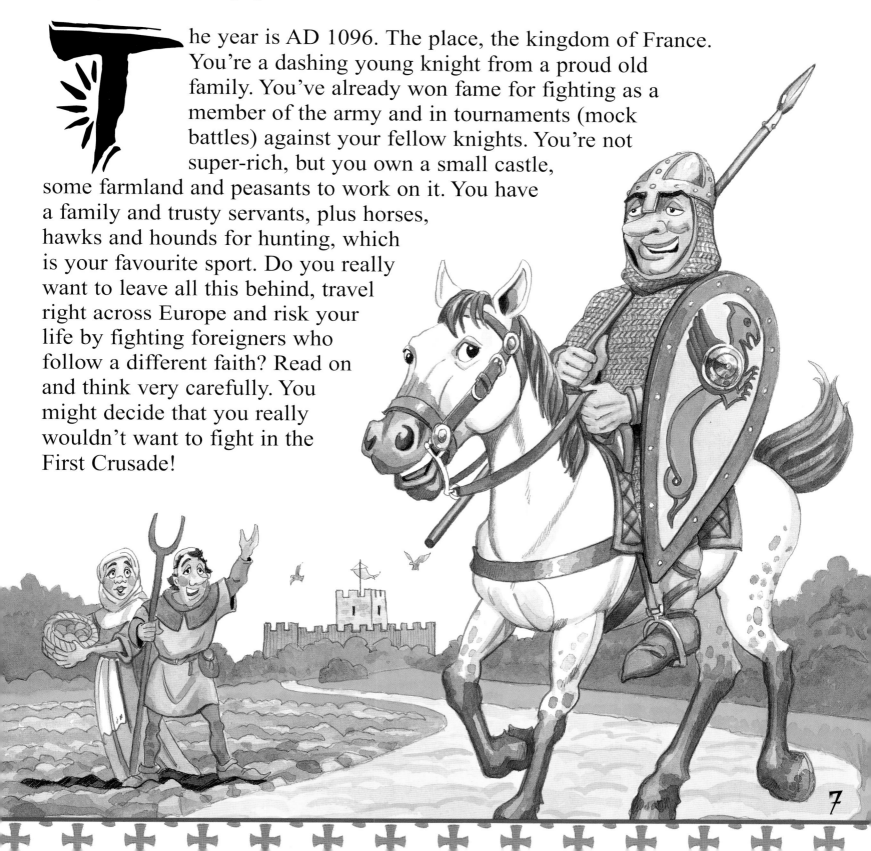

The year is AD 1096. The place, the kingdom of France. You're a dashing young knight from a proud old family. You've already won fame for fighting as a member of the army and in tournaments (mock battles) against your fellow knights. You're not super-rich, but you own a small castle, some farmland and peasants to work on it. You have a family and trusty servants, plus horses, hawks and hounds for hunting, which is your favourite sport. Do you really want to leave all this behind, travel right across Europe and risk your life by fighting foreigners who follow a different faith? Read on and think very carefully. You might decide that you really wouldn't want to fight in the First Crusade!

The Pope preaches

Pope Urban II is a man with a mission! He is leader of the Christian Church in western Europe and a forceful character who expects to be obeyed. For some time now he's had two great aims. He hopes to bring peace to war-torn Christian countries. And he's determined to defeat Turkish warriors in the Holy Land (the territory around the ancient city of Jerusalem, over 2,000 miles (3,200 kilometres) away, in the Middle East). Last year, as you know, Pope Urban made a special journey all through France. Towards the end, he preached a rousing sermon.

THE SELJUK TURKS (left) are Muslim warriors from Central Asia. Since 1071 they have ruled most of the Middle Eastern lands.

JERUSALEM is a holy city. It is very important to three great faiths: Judaism, Christianity and Islam.

THE SELJUKS have attacked Holy Land cities and challenged local Muslim rulers.

TRAVEL has become dangerous for local people, merchants and religious pilgrims.

Were you there, with thousands of other Frenchmen, to listen to Pope Urban? His message was simple – and startling. 'Stop fighting each other!' he commanded. 'Start a holy war against the Turks, instead!'

Handy hint

Do your duty and fight! It's what the Pope commands!

Defend the Church! Save the Holy City!

What's so special about Jerusalem?

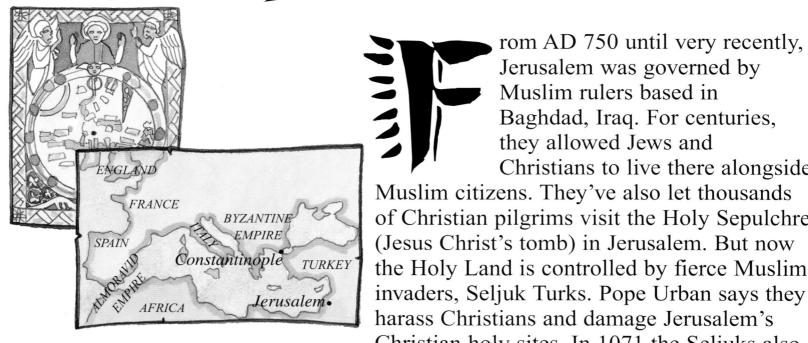

MEDIEVAL MAPS (above) show Jerusalem as the centre of the world. It's a favourite destination for Christian pilgrims. Over 10,000 visited the city from western Europe in 1065.

From AD 750 until very recently, Jerusalem was governed by Muslim rulers based in Baghdad, Iraq. For centuries, they allowed Jews and Christians to live there alongside Muslim citizens. They've also let thousands of Christian pilgrims visit the Holy Sepulchre (Jesus Christ's tomb) in Jerusalem. But now the Holy Land is controlled by fierce Muslim invaders, Seljuk Turks. Pope Urban says they harass Christians and damage Jerusalem's Christian holy sites. In 1071 the Seljuks also conquered a large part of the Byzantine Empire, a Christian state that rules eastern Europe and Turkey. Some people fear that, before long, the Seljuks might head west and conquer the rest of Europe, as well!

Holy sites

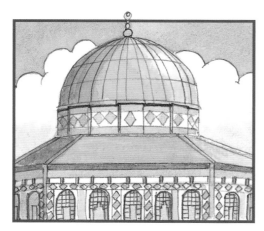

MUSLIMS honour Jerusalem because it was the place where the Prophet Muhammad received a revelation of heaven.

JEWISH PEOPLE honour Jerusalem as the site of their holiest temple and as their traditional home.

AS A CHRISTIAN KNIGHT you honour Jerusalem because Jesus preached there and died there on the Cross.

Handy hint

Pilgrims – be discreet! Don't boast about your faith when visiting Jerusalem.

MUSLIM CALIPH AL-HAKIM (above) was mentally ill. In 1009, he destroyed Jerusalem's Christian church on the site of Jesus's tomb.

TODAY, IN 1096, Pope Urban claims that Seljuks are attacking Jerusalem's Christian churches.

We used to get 7,000 Christian pilgrims – now, because of the war, none of them come!

Fight for God's forgiveness

GREED. Priests say that the love of money is the cause of all evil.

You are young, but you know that fighting is risky. You've seen hundreds of knights and foot soldiers die. Pope Urban's new holy war will be fought far away, against unknown enemies. If you win brave battles or perform daring deeds, you will gain riches and glory. But are they reward enough? The Pope has given another, better reason for joining his holy war. He has promised that God will forgive Christian soldiers' sins and reward them with a place in Heaven. Going to fight may be a good way of showing that you're sorry for being sinful and of escaping God's punishment when you die!

LUST.
A great temptation to a lively young man!

ENVY. You want to have the best of everything, like your rich neighbours.

GLUTTONY.
As a Frenchman, it's natural for you to appreciate good food!

ANGER. Life is full of things that may annoy you, but try to control your temper.

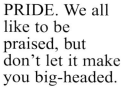

SLOTH. Don't be lazy. Make an effort! Hard work might be good for you.

PRIDE. We all like to be praised, but don't let it make you big-headed.

Take your weapons and armour

t costs a lot to equip a knight for battle. Can you afford to join the holy war? A long, heavy sword for slashing at enemies is essential, as is a sharp spear. You'll also need a mace (war club) for bashing them over the head and a dagger for stabbing. Don't leave home without your armour: a chain-mail tunic, a domed metal helmet and a big kite-shaped shield – the most useful design when fighting on horseback. Spurs – sharp metal points fixed to the heels of your shoes – will make your horse gallop faster if you press them into his sides. They are a sign of high rank and only knights can wear them.

A PADDED CAP worn under your helmet adds comfort and protection.

A LONG SURCOAT worn over your armour helps keep you cool in desert sun.

BIG BREECHES, padded with cotton, protect private parts and prevent saddle-sores!

A LONG, HOODED WOOLLEN CLOAK will keep you warm in winter and at night.

ONE WARHORSE is essential, two or three are better. You'll need baggage-horses too.

15

Preparing to leave

You have almost made up your mind to obey the Pope's commands and fight. But you don't want to leave your wife and family. If only they could come with you! But that would be dangerous for the children and – like other medieval women – your wife is not trained to fight. Anyway, she has far too many duties to be able to leave home. Even now, she is in charge of running your castle, keeping accounts, managing servants, ordering provisions, educating the children, entertaining important visitors and providing charity for poor peasants. While you're away, she will have to manage your farmland and will spend many hours praying for your safe return.

GIVE A PEP TALK to your eldest son. Tell him to be good and to look after the family.

RAISE CASH! You'll need a lot for food and travelling. Some knights borrow money for this. If they don't pay it back, they will lose their land.

ISSUE ORDERS! You may be away for a year or more. Make sure your servants know what to do.

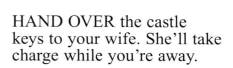

HAND OVER the castle keys to your wife. She'll take charge while you're away.

AT LONG LAST, YOU'VE DECIDED! You asked your wife for advice and she said 'Go!' She thinks it is your duty, but she'll miss you terribly.

I might never see them again!

Handy hint

Make a will! That way, you'll be sure that your sons will inherit your land.

Will you follow a hermit?

t is now April 1096 and you are faced with another difficult choice. Should you join the mob of ordinary people that has gathered together in Germany? It is led by two strange characters, Peter the Hermit (a holy man) and Walter Sans-Avoir (a French knight whose name means 'Walter the Penniless'). They are setting off for the Holy Land right now! But if you're wise, you will wait for a while and join an army led by an experienced military man.

Follow me and find God!

Or wait to be led by a lord?

GODFREY OF BOUILLON is determined and ruthless. His group includes his brothers Eustace and Baldwin.

BOHEMUND OF TARENTUM is a great warrior. He wants to conquer the Byzantines.

RAYMOND OF TOULOUSE wants to be king of Jerusalem. He has his wife with him!

"At 16 kilometres a day, I reckon we'll be marching most of the year!"

Handy hint

Be nice to the Byzantines! They could be useful allies.

ALL WARRIOR LORDS have their faults, but at least they know how to organise a march, plan a battle and lead a fight.

PRINCE HUGH of Vermandois is arrogant and foolish. He is also the brother of the King of France.

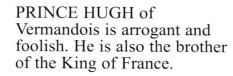

BISHOP ADHEMAR is a stern warrior. He wants to lead the Church in the Holy Land.

ROBERT OF NORMANDY is a pious man. He's borrowed money from his brother the King of England to pay for his journey.

19

Do you know where you're going?

You have no globe showing countries of the world, and no maps either. In fact, there are very few maps available and most of them are pretty inaccurate anyway. You have heard travellers' tales from pilgrims who have made the long journey to Jerusalem. You have also met merchants who have sailed to trade at ports all around the Mediterranean Sea. But you yourself are not an experienced traveller. You have always ridden on horseback and have never been more than 100 miles (160 kilometres) from home. You find it hard to believe that it might take months to travel from France to Jerusalem. And you have no idea of all the difficulties and dangers that lie in wait along the way!

A dangerous journey

LOOK OUT for puddles, deep ruts, loose stones and potholes! All roads have them.

MIND THE MUD! In some places it's so deep that you and your horse may sink without trace.

TAKE CARE on steep and narrow mountain paths! It's a long way to fall!

BANDITS AND ROBBERS lie in wait for travellers alongside many roads. They'll steal all your money and belongings, including your clothes, and leave you to die of cold.

YOUR FIRST TIME ON A SAILING SHIP. You'll discover it takes time to find your sea legs and stop being seasick!

Handy hint

Take a good pair of boots! You'll be travelling over rough ground, and doing a lot of walking!

Cheer up! The voyage only lasts six weeks!

MANY RIVERS have no bridges. You'll need to find a ferry-boat, or swim!

STEPPING STONES can be very slippery! If you fall in you'll be soaked to the skin.

Your horse isn't able to walk across stepping stones. He might fall and break a leg.

IN WINTER your route may be blocked by snowdrifts, or covered in ice.

IN SUMMER you'll suffer from the heat and dust, thirst and sunstroke!

21

Know your enemy

 our rivals, the Seljuk Turks, have conquered the Holy Land. They have a reputation as fearsome fighters, but they are not savages. They belong to a multicultural civilisation based in Central Asia. It combines ancient nomad traditions with ideas from Ancient Greece, Iran and India, all blended together with the faith of Islam. The Seljuks speak Turkish, a central Asian language, and dress in their own special style. They wear knee-length tunics and cloaks over baggy trousers and boots. The Seljuks have beards and moustaches and, sometimes, long, flowing hair. For battle, they put on armour made of little plates of metal, and pointed metal helmets with turbans wrapped around.

The Seljuk Turks

THE SELJUKS are Muslims who follow the Sunni (majority) branch of Islam. They pray five times a day.

LIKE YOU, Seljuk soldiers believe that they are fighting to defend their faith. They also want to conquer more land.

SELJUK CRAFTSMEN create beautiful rugs, silks, glassware and pottery. The Seljuks build tall tombs of decorative brick.

IN BATTLE, Seljuks ride up close on fast, nimble ponies, shoot with bows and arrows, then gallop out of harm's way.

Will you be cruel in Constantinople?

By now it is spring 1097. If you chose to follow Peter the Hermit, you may be dead already! Many of his followers have died from hunger and disease, or been killed in ambushes and accidents. Their route ran through Austria, Hungary and Serbia to Byzantine Empire lands. If you survived that journey, you may have died in a great battle against Seljuk warriors led by Kilij Arslan.

If, instead, you joined armies led by European lords, you may still be alive – but you should be ashamed of yourself! In January, you and your comrades ran wild through the streets of Constantinople, capital of the Byzantine Empire, in a disgraceful riot. It was caused by a stupid quarrel over food.

Or nasty in Nicea?

AFTER MONTHS ON THE MARCH, you Christian soldiers feel mean. You're tired, scared and suspicious. So when you arrive near the city of Nicea, you just lose control. You attack peaceful farming families, even though they are Christians, set fire to their homes and steal their food. But you quickly forget your shame after winning famous victories. You defeat Kilij Arslan twice, in May and July 1097.

Or ambitious in Edessa?

IF YOU CHOOSE to join the troop led by a lord called Baldwin of Boulogne, you will break away from the main Christian army, which is heading south towards Syria. Instead, you will march inland and take over the rich city of Edessa. Watch as Baldwin sets up a new Christian county (or state) there, with himself as ruler, in March 1098!

I hope it fits. Becoming ruler of Edessa has made him very big-headed!

Handy hint

Take extra care of your horse! By 1098, four out of every five knights' horses will have died!

25

Surround a city and survive a siege

I t is now October 1097 and if you are still alive you've done very well indeed. Unless you are heading inland to Edessa with Lord Baldwin of Boulogne (see page 25), you will have reached the Holy Land! But as part of the main Christian army, you face a tough time ahead. You have just arrived outside Antioch in Syria, one of the most important Muslim cities. Your commanders have set up camp around it and started a siege. They hope to stop all supplies of food and weapons from entering the city. The Muslims trapped inside its walls will either starve to death or be forced to surrender.

At Antioch

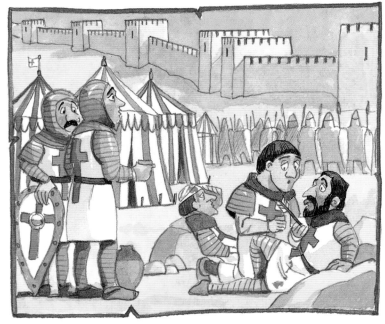

DISASTER! The Turks send an army to attack you and your fellow Christian soldiers. Now you're trapped! For seven months you can't get into Antioch and you can't run away.

SAVED BY A SPY! One of your army commanders – Bohemund – recruits an Armenian spy. He helps 60 Christian knights to break into Antioch. They open the gates and you and your soldiers rush in!

Siege warfare

ARMOURED TUNNELS (left) protect the miners, digging under city walls, from arrows shot by defenders high above.

Handy hint

Put your trust in miracles! At Antioch, a vision of the Holy Lance (spear) inspires soldiers to fight on.

Battering ram

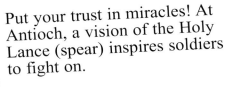

TALL SIEGE TOWERS help soldiers climb over walls, or shoot arrows into the city streets below.

MASSIVE BATTERING RAMS smash holes in walls, gates and towers.

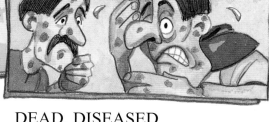

DEAD, DISEASED BODIES are thrown into enemy cities to spread germs – and fear!

MORE MUSLIM TROOPS arrive and surround Antioch. Now you're trapped inside the city! Conditions are terrible: no food, bad water, and dead bodies everywhere.

YOU ATTACK and the Muslim army rides away! You don't know this yet, but your victory will be short-lived – another Muslim army is on its way, and then it will be your turn to be besieged.

Reaching Jerusalem

ver 60,000 Christians set off from Europe to fight in the Holy Land. Now, in December 1098, only 20,000 are still alive. The surviving soldiers, including you, are starving and shivering in the cold. There are even rumours of cannibalism among some fighting men! But you don't turn back. In the spring, when the weather improves, you help lead the Christian army south, to reach Jerusalem. After yet another gruelling siege, on 15 July 1099, you break through its walls and set foot on its holy ground.

Onwards to Jerusalem

TURKEY

MEDITERRANEAN SEA

• Antioch

• Tyre

• Jerusalem

JERUSALEM IS OCCUPIED by Muslims from Egypt, who conquered it in 1098. You set up your siege engines and prepare to attack its walls.

BEFORE BESIEGING JERUSALEM, the Christian army walks round and round its walls. This is meant to show sorrow for their sins.

THE CHRISTIAN SOLDIERS are led by bishops and priests, chanting prayers and singing hymns.

THE LAND IS PARCHED around Jerusalem. In the summer heat the Christian troops can't find enough water to drink.

AFTER ENTERING JERUSALEM, horrible events take place. Christian troops massacre all the Muslim men, women and children they can find. The troops also attack Muslim buildings in revenge for the Seljuk damage to Christian ones.

Handy hint

Don't drink the water! The Muslim defenders of Jerusalem have poisoned wells and streams nearby, to kill attackers.

29

Will you ever return home?

After helping to capture Jerusalem, what will you do? Will you once again kiss your wife and children and live peacefully in your castle? Only if you are very lucky! Your war lasted for three years, from 1096 to 1099. It was just the first of many Crusades (Christian wars) that started because of religion. In all these wars, many soldiers, just like you, believed they were doing their duty and risked their lives for their faith. Others joined the wars because of greed, ambition or prejudice. But the Crusades caused tremendous suffering and led to bitterness and misunderstanding between different peoples that still continues today.

What happens next?

WILL YOU RISK the dangerous overland journey home, or chance a long voyage back to France by sea? Both are very hazardous – many returning Christian soldiers die this way.

MIGHT YOU STAY in the Holy Land with your victorious war-leaders and help them run a new Christian kingdom, ruled from Jerusalem?

WILL YOU DIE a slow, painful death from infected battle injuries? Or perhaps perish in an enemy prison from cold, hunger and thirst?

How will you be remembered?

Learn from what you've seen! Medieval Muslim peoples have great artistic skills and advanced science, maths, medicine and technology.

AS A CRUSADER? The cross-shaped badge worn by Christian soldiers will give your war – and others like it – a special new name. In about a hundred years from now (around AD 1200) chroniclers will start to call them 'Wars of the Cross' or 'Crusades'.

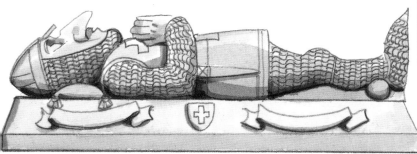

HONOURED AS A HERO? Your friends and family think you are a hero for fighting in the Holy Land. So they will pay for a fine tomb when you die. It will be topped with a lifelike carved statue so people will remember you.

REMEMBERED FOR THE WRONG REASONS? Will your name mean only terror to peaceful people in the Holy Land? Will they tell their children sad stories about the suffering caused by the war?

Avoid being in a Medieval Castle!

Introduction

You're a country girl in 13th-century England. You're used to a farming life, so you really think you're in luck when you get the chance to work in the local castle. You imagine you'll be mingling with lords and ladies – the sort of grand people who speak French to each other!

But there's trouble ahead. The year is 1215 and King John is in a power struggle with his barons. They're lords of Norman-French descent who have been the ruling class in England since the Normans conquered it, a century and a half ago.

The king has been forced to sign an agreement with the barons – the Magna Carta or Great Charter – which gives them the right to overrule the king. But John shows no sign of sticking to the agreement. When some of the angry barons rebel, you find yourself caught up in a terrible siege.

The ruins of Rochester castle, Kent, as they are today. Our tale is based on the true story of the siege of Rochester castle in 1215.

The castle across the river

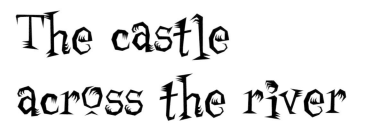

You're helping with the harvest but you're dreaming of the castle. You'll be living there soon! Your father has got you a job there. These villeins (peasant farmers) don't like your father. As bailiff of the castle estate, his job is to see that they work as hard as possible for the lord of the castle.

THE BAILIFF makes the villeins work the lord's land, in return for the right to use some of the land for themselves.

HE DEALS with the reeve (the spokesman for the villeins) and the hayward (who mends fences and rounds up strays).

Perhaps I'll have a lovely room with a view of the river...

MUCH of the villeins' own harvest goes to the lord as rent. This poor woman is paying her rent in eggs – only the rich use money.

MOST VILLEIN HOMES have just two rooms; one of them is for the animals. Your father's house is much grander – it has three rooms!

Handy hint

Five men can harvest two acres (0.8 hectare) in a day, as every bailiff knows. Don't let them take longer – they're just being lazy.

Rochester castle

Rochester cathedral

Why would they want *her* in the castle?

I suppose she thinks she's better than us.

In the bailey

It's the great day! You've come with your father to the castle. When you pass through its gate into the bailey – that's the area inside the castle walls – you're amazed to find that it's just like a busy village inside. There are stables, barracks, and all sorts of other wooden buildings around the walls. Everything you need to live on is here. There's a small farm with vegetable plots, cow sheds, a poultry yard and a dairy. In the big central space, men-at-arms are being drilled.

WHILE YOUR father talks with the marshal (he's head of military supplies), you watch the farrier shoeing a huge warhorse. 'A warhorse is the most expensive thing a knight has to buy,' he tells you.

Gatehouse

I thought this was a friendly match!

MEN-AT-ARMS (soldiers who are not knights) wrestle to keep fit while they're not on guard duty. When a lord needs warriors he summons knights from their estates.

So... What's your excuse?

THESE VILLEINS are accused of grinding their corn at home instead of paying to have it ground at the lord's mill. They'll be tried by the sheriff at his court in the castle.

Key to the bailey:

(Note: The wooden buildings have not survived – we can only guess what they were like.)

1 Barracks
2 Armoury
3 Smithy
4 Stables
5 Kennels
6 Almonry
7 Storage barn
8 Chapel and belfry
9 Guesthouse
10 Hall and buttery
11 Kitchen
12 Bakehouse
13 Brewhouse
14 Laundry
15 Dispensary
16 Chandlery
17 Poultry yard
18 Cattle shed
19 Dairy
20 Hay barn
21 Tool and wagon shed

Handy hint

A well-stocked bailey is no use if attackers can get in. Protect it with a strong gatehouse and a drawbridge over a moat.

Keep

Exercise yard

Kitchen garden

Cattle yard

Orchard

Outer wall or curtain wall

The Keep

Archbishop's private apartments

Archbishop's private chapel

Furniture under wraps

Trestle table packed away

Archbishop's state rooms

Sheriff's court in the Great Hall

Haven't I seen you here before?

Storage rooms at ground level

A cutaway view of the castle keep.

'Will I be seeing the lord of the castle?' you ask nervously when you reach the keep. Your father laughs. 'No, he's much too grand. He's the Lord Archbishop of Canterbury – the most important churchman in the country. He's hardly ever here. The castle is run by his deputy, the Constable. He's an important baron and you will be serving his wife.'

Your new job

YOUR FATHER leaves you with the chamberlain, a busy man in charge of household affairs. He takes you to the Great Chamber where the ladies spend the day. The Constable's wife lives like a great lady, with damsels (ladies-in-waiting) to wait on her. One of the older ladies explains your duties. Clearly she doesn't think much of you. 'You need new clothes,' she says. 'We don't want ragamuffins. You'll get some as Christmas pay. Till then you'll wear cast-offs.'

If attackers ever break into the bailey, the castle dwellers can shut themselves safe and snug inside the keep. Its walls are thick, its windows small and high, and its entry well protected. Its cellars are stocked with food and weapons, and it has its own well. The first floor, where the Constable lives, is split by a wall into two large rooms: the Hall, where he conducts business, and the Great Chamber for family use. The Archbishop's rooms above are under wraps until he comes.

Handy hint

Medieval advice to an untrained servant: 'Do not claw your back as if you were after a flea, or stroke your hair as if you sought a louse.'

And stand up straight when I'm talking to you!

She was just the same when I started working here.

I want to go home.

A castle day

At noon everyone eats in the hall in the bailey. The Constable, his lady and the household officials sit at the 'high table' at the top end of the hall. Everybody else sits at trestle tables down the length of the hall, with the more important people nearer the top. You're right at the bottom, next to a smug-looking page. He helps himself to stew, spooning it onto the trencher of bread in front of him. You copy him, so he'll think you know how to behave. Then he starts talking French – just to embarrass you!

Bonjour.

How many robes has she got?

COCKCROW. Horror! Last night you forgot to get water for the ladies' morning wash. You sneak to the indoor well in the hall while the men are still putting away their beds – strictly forbidden!

NEXT you help the ladies dress. You liven up the fire and warm their clothes in front of it. You help them pull on their hose (stockings) and hold the mirror while they do their hair.

YOU PUT the daytime cover on her ladyship's bed, tie back its curtains and put away the maids' truckle beds. Then you go to Mass, which everyone attends in the bailey chapel.

THE ELDERLY, sour-tempered damsel takes you to the wardrobe, a room where clothes are stored. Here you spend the morning cleaning fur-lined robes by rubbing them with bran.

Handy hint

Don't bite your bread roll; break a piece off. Leftovers go to the poor, and they don't want your teeth marks!

IN THE AFTERNOON the ladies hunt with falcons. The Constable's Lady keeps hers in the Great Chamber. You have to sweep up its droppings and put clean rushes on the floor.

EVERY SPARE moment must be spent spinning – twisting wool into thread. When the ladies return, you are beaten with your own distaff for letting the dog foul the rushes.

THE LADY has a bath quite often – once a month or so – in a big half-barrel which is lined with cloth in case of splinters. You have to keep topping it up with hot water.

YOU SLEEP on a straw pallet at the draughtier end of the room. From where you lie there's a strong whiff from the garderobe (toilet). It's worse than your outdoor privy at home.

From page to Knight

EVERY PAGE hopes to become a squire – and every squire hopes to become a knight.

THE NIGHT before the knighting ceremony, the squire takes a bath and dresses in white to symbolise his purity of spirit.

HE SPENDS all night praying in the chapel. Next morning he makes his confession to the priest and hears Mass.

THE PRIEST blesses the squire's sword. The lord then 'dubs' him knight by striking him on the shoulder with this same sword.

That smug page is so full of himself, you could kick him.

'My father is a baron and lives in a castle,' he tells you, 'so of course he's sent me away from home to get a good tough education. I've lived here since I was seven. I'm learning to be a knight, and when I'm fourteen they'll make me a squire like my brother. He is squire to the Constable. He serves him at table, looks after his horse and arms, and rides with him into battle. One day he'll be a knight.'

You've seen the page training in the bailey, and you think you'd make a much better squire than him. When he rode at the quintain he was much too slow and the weight swung round and hit him.

Did you ever see anything like it?

AFTER A FINAL blessing everyone celebrates. These ceremonies are not essential. A lord can reward a brave man by dubbing him knight in the thick of battle.

IN PEACETIME, knights hold practice fights called *mêlées*. There are no rules – they just attack each other, and some get killed.

Clannng!

Handy hint

A squire should keep his knight's armour sparkling by rolling it in a barrel of sand, then polishing it with a wad of horsetail plant.

Thwack!

The quintain is a swivelling target mounted on a post. It's used to practise charging with a lance.

The sandbag adds weight to the target, so you have to hit it pretty hard. Then you're supposed to get out of the way before the bag swings round.

Knight in shining armour? Damsel in distress, more like!

The Lord comes to stay

The Lord Archbishop is on his way! Everyone is in a rush, sorting out stabling, rooms and food for the huge household of officials and servants he'll be bringing with him. Great lords always travel like this. They have several homes and move from one to another. If they stayed put, their household would soon exhaust the local food supply. So they move on, taking their possessions with them. The archbishop brings his clothes, knock-down furniture, state hangings, bed covers, household linen, chapel furnishings, buttery and kitchen equipment, church candles and barrels of best French wine.

Fit for a lord?

THE ARCHBISHOP'S officials arrive some days ahead to see that his rooms are in order. Does the chimney still smoke; do the shutters fit; are the hangings up?

That won't do!

HIS STEWARD insists that the Archbishop's chamber needs whitewashing, and there must be a better chest for displaying his gold dishes when they arrive.

HIS BAKER comes to make the Archbishop's favourite French bread. He's far too grand to cook it himself, of course – he gives orders to the castle staff.

Handy hint

Be prepared for a big crowd at the almonry, where charity is given to the poor. When there's a banquet, beggars flock from far and wide.

IN HIS STATE CHAMBER, the Archbishop is holding a banquet for local nobles. The walls are hung with painted cloths and a state canopy hangs over his throne. The high table is elegantly draped and set with gold plates. Trumpeters herald each course and his carver kneels before him, waiting to serve. Musicians play in the gallery.

Rebel barons

LONDONERS are backing the rebels at the moment – but if John returns with a foreign army they may be forced to change their minds.

THE CONSTABLE welcomes the barons.

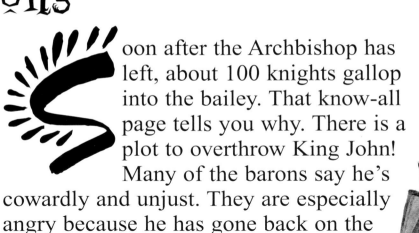

Soon after the Archbishop has left, about 100 knights gallop into the bailey. That know-all page tells you why. There is a plot to overthrow King John! Many of the barons say he's cowardly and unjust. They are especially angry because he has gone back on the promises he made in Magna Carta.

John is at Dover on the south coast, waiting for foreign help. Rochester castle controls the route from Dover to London, so the Archbishop is letting the barons take over the castle to stop the King returning to the capital.

Squawk!

Er... that's it!

BUT THE CASTLE is not ready for more visitors so soon after the Archbishop's visit! There are hardly any weapons in the armoury.

Plip!

THERE'S NOT much food or wine in the cellars, either. Entertaining the Archbishop has used up all the reserves.

THE REBELS raid the city of Rochester, forcing terrified citizens to part with their supplies at swordpoint.

A MESSENGER gallops in to warn the rebels that the King is on his way with a huge army to attack the castle.

47

The bridge

The rebels know they'll be outnumbered, but they're not going to surrender. They're sure the barons in London will soon send help. Till then they must prepare for a siege, so the Constable has ordered everyone on the castle's estate to bring in food at once. You've been sent home to fetch whatever your family can spare. Returning to the castle, you are horrified to find that the King's men are already there, in boats, setting fire to the struts of the bridge!

River Medway

I hope we can get back in.

What is a siege?

The idea of a siege is to surround the castle with troops so that the defenders cannot get out, or bring supplies into the castle. Once they have run out of food, they will have to surrender. Destroying the bridge will cut the castle off from the west.

THE BOATS have been beaten off, but your heart is in your mouth. Will the bridge still support the horse, the cow and you?

Creak!

SOON THE attackers are back in greater numbers. They destroy the bridge and take over the city.

I hope we can't.

Handy hint

In a siege, you need a water supply that the enemy can't cut off. Otherwise you may have to drink urine or horse's blood.

KING JOHN uses the cathedral as a stable for his horses. The clergy are horrified.

SAFELY BACK in the castle, you see that the hill overlooking the bailey is covered with tents and armed men. Will you be safe for long?

Casualties

The siege is in its second week now. Scared and exhausted, you're in the keep, digging crossbow bolts out of men's flesh and binding their wounds. There are a thousand of the King's men outside, firing crossbows at the defenders on the outer walls and trying to put up scaling ladders.

Worse still, five mighty trebuchets are hurling rocks into the bailey, smashing its wooden buildings to bits and pounding the stone walls.

A TREBUCHET works like a see-saw. A huge boulder is placed in the sling. Then the sling arm is pulled down with a winch. When the arm is let go, the massive weight on the other end makes it shoot up again, hurling the boulder into the air.

Sling

Sling arm

Trebuchet

Winch

Weight (box of boulders)

The wall's down!

They're getting into the bailey!

A CONSTANT RAIN of boulders on one part of the wall produces first a crack, then a crumbling, then collapse.

Don't worry about him, dear. At least he's still well enough to scream.

Handy hint

Spiral stairs must turn clockwise. That gives you elbow-room (if you're right-handed) to swing your sword against an attacker climbing up towards you.

YOU THROW a firepot yourself, just to show that useless page, struggling with his crossbow, that you can fight too.

HE'S YANKED the bowstring into place at last! He takes aim at someone who looks very like the King. But a rebel knight reminds him that it would be a sin to kill an anointed king – even a bad one.

Urgh!

Pan!

DEFENDERS on the roof of the keep are calling for firepots (pottery bombs filled with tar and lighted rags) to drop on the enemy below.

Oh... yes... I suppose so.

51

The tower collapses

I t's week five of the siege. Everybody who escaped death when the bailey fell has fled to the keep. Conditions here are dreadful. People are crowded in, with barely room to lie down to sleep, and very soon the food will run out. The trebuchets are still pounding, though surely they can't make much of a dent in the walls of the keep – they are nearly 4 metres thick. The enemy's ladders are useless too: the keep is much too high to scale. Perhaps you can hold out until help arrives from London – or perhaps not...

Ooh-er!

ONE DAY, while dressing wounds in the south tower of the keep, you notice that the surface of the water in a storage jar is quivering. What could be making the tower vibrate? You decide to raise the alarm.

THE TOWER is being mined! The King's men are digging a tunnel underneath the base of the tower. Its timber roof is held up by wooden props.

Arrow slit

Baskets of earth

Wooden shelter covered with animal hides

Pit props

Talus (stone ramp to protect base of wall)

THE MINERS carry props in and take earth out under a protective shelter.

Mine

52

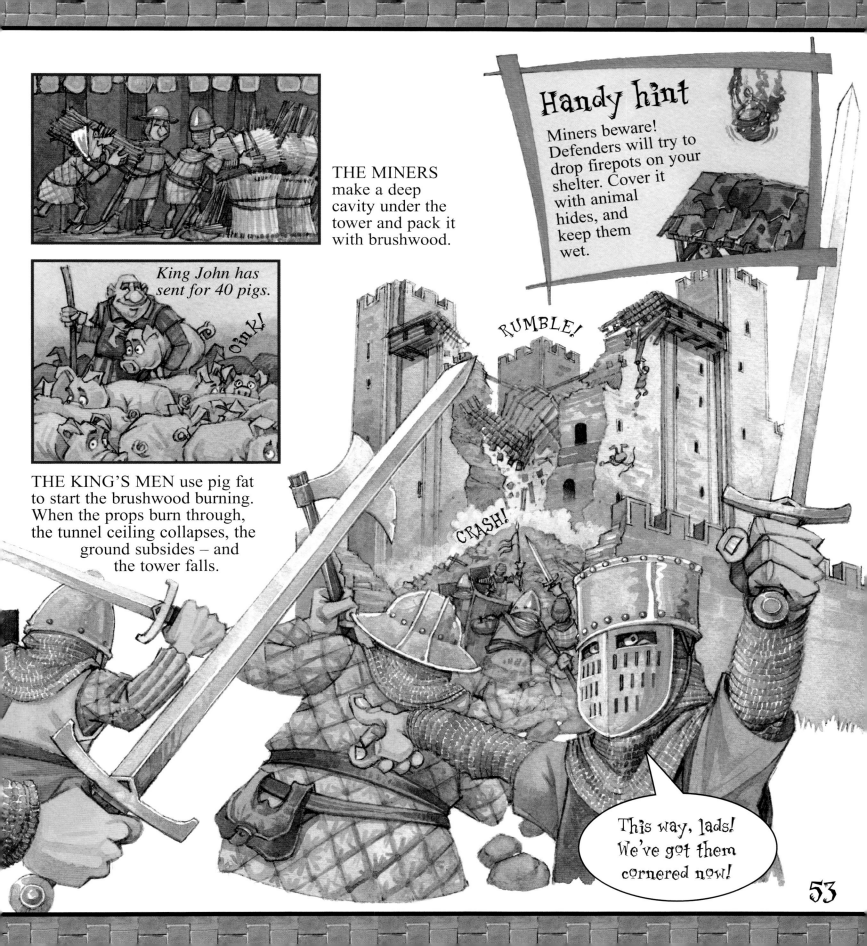

THE MINERS make a deep cavity under the tower and pack it with brushwood.

Handy hint

Miners beware! Defenders will try to drop firepots on your shelter. Cover it with animal hides, and keep them wet.

King John has sent for 40 pigs.

Oink!

THE KING'S MEN use pig fat to start the brushwood burning. When the props burn through, the tunnel ceiling collapses, the ground subsides – and the tower falls.

RUMBLE!

CRASH!

This way, lads! We've got them cornered now!

Holding out in the Keep

A quarter of the keep has crashed to the ground. The King's men have poured into the Great Chamber but they cannot get control of the whole keep. The rebels have barred the connecting doors between the Chamber and the Hall and are fighting on from there. They have almost no food left, and nothing to drink but water – a liquid that's considered fit only to wash in. You are simmering a few scraps of horsemeat when you see the door leading to the floor above begin to open. John's men are trying to get in from upstairs! The guard is too quick for them this time, but how much longer can the rebels hold out?

If you can't fight, you can't eat!

...that's what I heard!

The swine!

THERE'S NOT enough food to go round, so the rebels force everyone who cannot fight to leave – even though they are bound to be captured by the enemy.

YOU DON'T WANT to be flung to the enemy so you hide as best you can. By the time you're noticed, no-one has time to bother with you.

YOU HEAR what happened to the ones who did go: John had their hands and feet cut off!

Goodbye to the castle

KING JOHN is thinking of celebrating his victory by having every one of the rebels hanged.

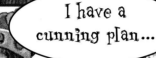

Nobody messes with me!

Starvation finally forces the rebels to surrender, after nearly two months of bitter siege. By this time you hardly care what happens; the enemy will kill you if the hunger doesn't. Luckily you are far too lowly for anyone to bother with you. Even the rebels are spared by the King's greed and cowardice; he's afraid that if he punishes the barons now, they'll get their own back later. He seizes the castle and staffs it with people loyal to himself.

I have a cunning plan...

Don't you worry about them, my girl – serves the blighters right!

BUT A FOREIGN captain has a better idea: the King should give each of his cronies a rebel to hold for ransom (keeping the most valuable for himself, of course).

THE KING still wants a bit of fun, so he hangs just one crossbowman, on grounds of ingratitude: the man had been raised in the royal household, so he ought to have been loyal.

Pig fat! They used pig fat!

Now your father is no longer bailiff and you're back home working on the land. You feel sorry for that wretched line of rebels being led off to moulder in castle prisons for who knows how long. What a joy to think you need never set foot in a castle again!

Burp!

Handy hint

Don't let an important captive go too cheaply. The longer you hold on to him, the more his family may be willing to fork out for him.

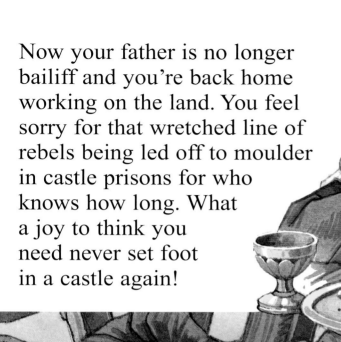

What came next?

WAR BETWEEN the King and the barons continued. But in 1216 John fell ill and died after overeating at a dinner given in his honour.

JOHN'S NINE-YEAR-OLD SON became King Henry III. He wisely made peace with the barons by giving back most of the rights that John had taken from them.

IN 1227 Rochester castle was repaired. The collapsed corner of the keep was given a modern round tower in place of the old square one. Round towers have no corners for the enemy to hide behind.

Avoid working on a Medieval Cathedral!

Introduction

Hello there! Welcome to Canterbury! It's an ancient city and home to England's most important cathedral. Travellers come from far and wide to see it.

Come and meet my grandson. Over here, lad, and say hello! He'll be twelve next birthday – born around 1370, if my memory's right. Soon it will be time for him to start work.

Have you chosen a career yet, laddie? Eh? Eh? You want to be a builder, like your father and like me, your old grandpapa? Well, it's a good job, the pay's not bad, and you could work with us, of course. But what's that you say? You want to be an expert, top-class, the best...

You want to be a cathedral builder?

A grand tradition

So you think everyday buildings are boring and dull – just plain walls and windows and doorways? Well, cathedrals are certainly much more exciting. They're designed in the latest, daring styles and use only the very best materials. And, of course, they're always being made bigger and more beautiful.

What are cathedrals for? Why, surely you know that! They're huge, rich churches, where Christians worship God and think about Heaven. And they're also bases for busy, bossy bishops.

Cathedral building would be a thrilling job, but, believe me, it's not easy. You'd need years of training and hard work, as well as natural talent. Do you think you're ready for that challenge?

Durham, England
c.1093–1133

Canterbury

YOU LIVE HERE

Notre Dame, Paris, France
c.1163–1240

Santiago de Compostela, Spain
c.1075–1128

What is a cathedral?

HOLY THRONE. The word *cathedral* comes from *cathedra*, the Latin (and Greek) name for a bishop's throne.

HOUSE OF GOD. To Christians, cathedrals are full of God's Holy Spirit. They are beautiful, holy places to say prayers.

STATUS SYMBOL. Grand and glorious, cathedrals are prestige buildings. Every big city wants to have one.

Cathedrals are the finest buildings in Europe, magnificently decorated with carvings, coloured glass, glittering jewels and sculptures. They don't all look the same: each is a unique, inspiring work of art. Here are just a few of the most famous.

Speyer, Germany c.1030–1100

St Mark's, Venice, Italy c.832–1250

Pisa, Italy c.1030–1250

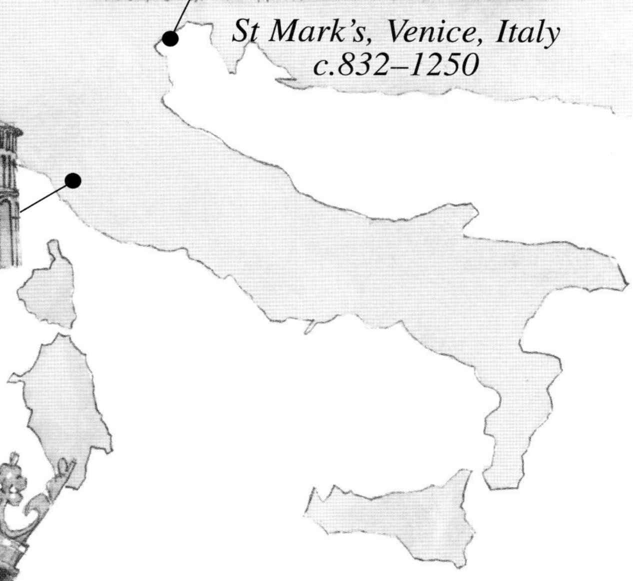

Handy hint

Build with the best! Most people live in fragile timber buildings that don't last long. But cathedrals are made of stone, and designed to last for ever!

BAND OF BROTHERS. Some cathedrals also have a monastery attached. Brotherhoods of monks live there, devoting their lives to God. They take part in cathedral prayers and sing in cathedral choirs.

ROYAL CONNECTIONS. Kings are crowned in cathedrals. They hope that God will help them rule, and protect them.

The story so far

BY THE 14th CENTURY, Canterbury Cathedral already has a history stretching back hundreds of years.

1. c. AD 597–602. First cathedral built by St Augustine using remains of old Roman church; later rebuilt twice. Burned down by Vikings in 1011 (they later murder the archbishop, St Alphege); rebuilt again by 1038.

2. c.1067–1077. Cathedral again destroyed by fire, and replaced by new-style building planned by Archbishop Lanfranc, from France.

3. c.1098–1130. Archbishop St Anselm adds buildings decorated in Italian, Greek and Muslim styles, and a crypt (hidden cellar).

Long-term project

ell me, my lad, how big is our house? Yes, four rooms, an attic and a workshop. And we are well off; most people nowadays live in cottages with one or two rooms.

Now, compare those homes with Canterbury Cathedral over there, towering above them. It's gigantic! It has pillars and arches, porches and niches, vast windows, steep roofs – and much more! Just think how complicated it was to design each part – and how long it took to construct them all! Cathedral-building takes centuries. It's a very slow process, aiming for perfection!

4. c.1174–1180. Another fire, and more rebuilding. A second crypt is added, plus new chapels. One houses the shrine of St Thomas Becket (see page 76).

5. c.1377–1410. The nave (main hall) of the cathedral is to be replaced by a splendid new one, with wonderful arches and carvings and a vaulted roof (see page 73).

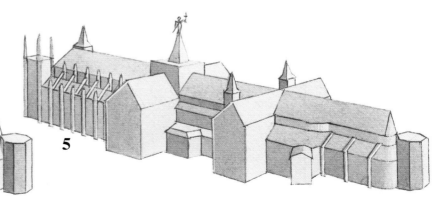

Angel Steeple

Canterbury Cathedral is 160 metres long, 47 metres wide and 72 metres high to the tip of its Angel Steeple.

Handy hint

Make friends with the rich and famous! New buildings at Canterbury are being paid for by a wealthy well-wisher.

You won't see another one like it anywhere!

63

Are you a good team player?

Meet the team

DEVISER. Designs each new section of the cathedral building, and marks out full-size patterns on the floor for masons and carvers to follow.

It takes hundreds of people, all with different skills, to create a cathedral. If you want to share in their grand project, you must learn to work with them all. Learn to give and take, be cheerful and polite. If you help others, they'll help you! But if you're rude or lazy, expect big trouble.

All cathedral builders are respected for the quality of their work. Their skills and knowledge are essential. Which building craft will you choose to learn? None of them is easy!

Ow!

WOODCARVER (below). Uses razor-sharp tools to decorate doors, seats, screens and pulpits with wonderful shapes and patterns.

Aaargh!

QUARRYMAN. Hacks huge lumps of rock from cliffs and crags, and hammers them into rough slabs ready for the masons.

WOODWORKERS. Sawyers saw tall tree-trunks into neat planks. Joiners make doors and window frames. Skilled carpenters build rafters and scaffolding.

Wheeze!

MASON (left). Some masons shape rough-cut stone into precise building blocks. Others decorate them with carvings. It's a dusty job!

64

How's that window going to fit into this frame?

If you get shirty with me I'll report you to the guild!

Handy hint

Join a craftsman's guild. There's one for each trade. In most cities, you can't get a skilled job without being a guild member.

Do you have the muscle power?

In the 14th century there are no power tools or engines. You must construct buildings by hand, using simple technology and an enormous amount of muscle power. Cathedral builders must be tough, hardworking and strong!

He might have what it takes...

ROOFER (left). Covers wooden roofs with sheets of lead, or tiles made from slate or stone, to keep out rain and snow.

GLAZIER (below). Creates glorious windows using jagged pieces of coloured glass held in place by lead borders.

BELL-MAKER. Pours molten bronze into moulds dug in the ground to make clanging bells that call worshippers to the cathedral.

65

Learning on the job

Now you're for it!

You say you'd like to be a stonemason. That's a good idea, but, whatever skill you decide to learn, you'll need a master to teach you. For seven years, you must promise to study, work hard and obey him. You'll live in his house as an apprentice – part pupil, part servant. You'll run errands, watch your master work, and ask lots of questions. The master will teach you all you need to know, from roughly shaping stone to carving delicate details. When the apprenticeship ends, you'll be older and wiser, and you'll graduate as a journeyman. Then you can work for anyone you choose, and you'll be paid by the day.

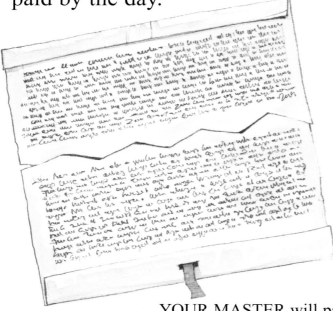

Crack!

YOUR MASTER will pay a scribe to write a contract recording his promise to train you. It's called an indenture, and is designed to be cut in two. Your master will keep one half, and your parents the other. The jagged cut edges can be fitted together to prove that each half is genuine.

SAY GOODBYE to your family! Now you must rely on yourself to survive. Quick wits and a willingness to learn will help you.

WORRIED AND CONFUSED by your new surroundings? Be brave! You'll soon get used to your master's busy household.

EXHAUSTED by days in the workshop? Your muscles will soon grow stronger and you'll learn many clever techniques.

Have mallet, will travel

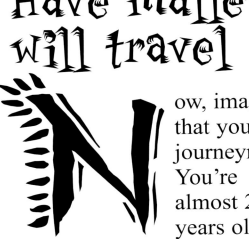

Now, imagine that you're a journeyman. You're almost 20 years old, with no home, no food, no money – and no master to guide you. You're trained, but have no experience.

Take an old man's advice, my lad! You need hard work, boring work – and plenty of it. Find whatever building job you can, and learn day by day. Build up your knowledge, your savings and your strength. Then, perhaps, a team of cathedral builders might be willing to employ you.

SAY GOODBYE to your master. He's taught you all he can. Now you must fend for yourself. Get ready – and get going!

Summer sun

Spring showers

Way-hey!

ROUSED BY NOISY REVELLERS at a busy roadside inn? Pull the blankets over your ears and try to ignore them!

Kyrie eleison!
(Lord, have mercy on us!)

Life on the road

LOOKING FOR LODGINGS at the local monastery? Remember, monks get up at midnight to chant their first prayers of the morning!

Autumn gales

AS A JOURNEYMAN, you may work on a project for days, weeks or years, until your task is completed. But then you'll need to find new work again, and quickly!
    Be prepared to walk miles between building sites – and to face tough travel conditions.

Handy hint

Make friends with senior stonemasons. They might shelter you in their _mansione_ (workroom and dormitory) on the building site.

WOOOOOoo

CROUCHED IN A CHURCH PORCH? Then you'll need strong nerves. Bats, owls and other creatures of the night have a habit of lurking there.

Wakey wakey!

Snort!

Winter snows

SEEKING SHELTER with peasants? Poor families bring their livestock indoors – and some creatures can get _far_ too close for comfort!

BEDDED DOWN IN A BARN? Then beware of the bull and other big animals sheltering there. They may not welcome sharing their space with sleepy strangers!

69

Practice makes perfect

Think ahead ten more years. You've survived as a travelling journeyman. It's been a tough life, but you've learned a lot from your workmates and from the sights you've seen on your travels. Your next step will be to apply for a job on site at Canterbury Cathedral.

But what's this splendid statue you've been working on secretly? Aha! It's your test-piece! I hope the craftsmen's jury likes it, because, if they do, you'll qualify as a proper master mason. You'll win prestige, more money, and respect from your friends and neighbours. Even more important, you'll get the chance to work on all kinds of cathedral stonework.

Will you pass the test?

A JURY of expert stonemasons will examine your test sculpture. Will they find fault and reject it – or praise it as your masterpiece?

GARGOYLES. These funny, scary faces (1) hide pipes that carry rainwater away from the walls and roofs.

BUTTRESSES (2) prevent high walls from leaning outwards.

STATUES of favourite saints (3) remind worshippers of Heaven.

ARCHES (4) hold up roofs and floors. Until around 1150, arches were made wide and rounded. Now, in the 1380s, they are narrow and pointed.

PILLARS support the arches. Most have decorated capitals at the top (5). Their shafts (uprights) may be carved to look like narrow columns side by side (6). Sometimes they are multi-coloured.

CARVED FRIEZES decorate the walls, inside and out (7).

STONE SLABS OR TILES cover the floor (8). There might also be a maze – a symbol of the soul's search for God.

Of course, it's a bit modern for my taste.

Nice work, though.

Do you think you could do that?

Just let me try!

Handy hint

Read the 'Poor Man's Bible'. That's the name for glowing stained-glass windows that tell Bible stories in pictures.

Shining example

Henry Yevele, the greatest master mason in England, arrived in Canterbury not long ago (c.1377) to work on the cathedral's new nave and monks' cloisters (courtyard). Yevele is already famous for building royal palaces and castles. So aim high – watch and copy him. It's the chance of a lifetime!

Grand designs

What next? Why not apply to help a famous master mason design a new chapel? If you get that job, you really will have reached the top of your profession!*

You'll have big responsibilities, too. Design mistakes can lead to terrible disasters. Have you heard of Ely Cathedral? In 1322, a badly designed stone tower crashed through its roof to the floor!

With luck, your new master will show you how to create exciting new designs. You'll study old buildings, make lots of measurements, and draw sketches. Some masons base their plans on mysterious mathematical calculations. They say that these contain holy secrets!

* It's the 14th century, and architects have not yet been invented.

Dual purpose

Flying buttress

Nave wall

MANY CATHEDRAL FEATURES are designed with a double purpose: to be useful *and* look good. Graceful 'flying buttresses' support walls without blocking the light from the windows.

KEEP A SKETCHBOOK, as French artist Villard de Honnecourt did in the 13th century.

BE BOLD! EXPERIMENT! Make trial drawings of your own building plans on a drawing-floor covered with wet plaster.

SLIM PINNACLES add weight to stonework to make it more stable.

Pinnacle

Top of buttress

RIB-VAULTING spreads the weight of the celling and carries it down to the ground.

Vault

Ribs

Pillars

We'll have to get the builders in again.

Handy hint

Make good foundations, or your building will never stand straight. Look at the famous Leaning Tower at Pisa Cathedral in Italy. It's built on sand!

Ely Cathedral, 1322: The central tower gives way, after standing for 200 years. It's lucky that no-one's killed.

73

Health and safety

I f you become a master mason yourself, it'll be your job to plan and manage all the different stages of the building. You must organise your masons: some will 'set out' (make templates for others to copy); others, less skilled, will saw and 'bank' (rough-cut) blocks into shape, ready for expert carver-masons to create the finished stonework. You must also give orders to the other craftsmen on site – and keep tight control of the budget!

At times, you'll get tired and stressed, but don't put your own life in danger. Remember what happened to master mason William of Sens, right here in Canterbury. He climbed 15 metres up to examine some stonework – and fell off the scaffolding!

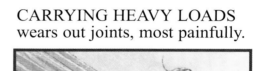

DUST stings eyes, scratches noses, tickles throats and chokes lungs.

CARRYING HEAVY LOADS wears out joints, most painfully.

BACKACHE comes from a life spent crouched over carvings.

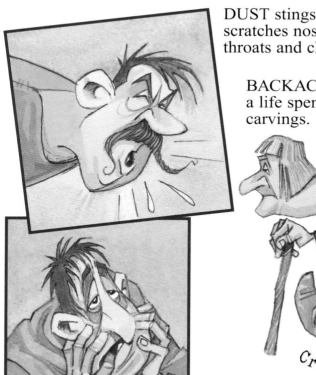

Creak

POISONOUS LEAD makes roofers and glaziers very, very ill.

GLASS FURNACES glow red-hot. They burn and blister. Ow!

Retired hurt

At first, William of Sens tried to keep on working from his sickbed. But he was too ill, and soon left Canterbury for France, his homeland. He died there in 1180, a year after his accident. His designs were completed by a new master mason, William the Englishman, in 1184.

Handy hint

Carry an amber amulet (charm). According to Arab doctors – some of the best in the 14th century – it will prevent rheumatism.

Where'd he go?

Aaaaargh!

Dare you argue with an abbot?

Are you courteous, tactful, smooth-talking, clear-headed, calm – and strong-minded? You'll need all these qualities when the time comes to talk to the people who pay for cathedral buildings. They range from kings, queens and local landowners to senior priests and abbots (heads of monasteries). Most will have travelled to Europe and seen fascinating buildings in foreign lands. They may want you to copy them.

All these rich, powerful people are used to getting their own way. They don't like to be contradicted! But you must persuade them that your plan is the best.

Bothersome bishops

CHURCHMEN often have strong views. In 1170, Canterbury's own archbishop, Thomas Becket, was murdered in the cathedral by royal soldiers after a quarrel with King Henry II. Now Becket's buried close to where he died, in a beautiful new chapel.

Local worthies

LEADING LOCAL PEOPLE – lords and ladies, mayors and merchants (left) – are very proud of 'their' cathedral. They are always willing to give money, but like to be consulted in return. Don't hurt their feelings!

Handy hint

Be trustworthy. William the Englishman (see page 75) got the job because he was 'acute [clever] and honest'.

There he goes again...

It's got to be better than anything the French have got.

Clever machines

Sheerlegs (a type of crane)

A LEWIS grabs blocks of stone like a giant pair of pincers; a sheerlegs or treadmill crane winds rope round and round to lift the load.

SOME LOADS of stone or timber are far too heavy to be moved by human muscles alone. Oxen or bullocks can be stubborn and awkward – but they're extremely powerful!

Counterweight for stability

Rope drum

Treadmill

Lewis

Ox power

Only the best will do

s master mason, it will also be your job to find building stone for the cathedral, and get it transported to the building site. That's no easy task! The stone for Canterbury comes all the way from Caen in northern France. It has to be hewn into blocks at the quarry, taken by ox-cart to the coast, loaded on ships and ferried across the English Channel, transferred to river barges, then carried on ox-carts (again) for the last mile or two.

Why go to all that trouble? Because Caen stone is some of the best in the world. It's limestone, with a smooth, fine texture and a lovely pale cream colour. And it's what masons call 'freestone', which means it can be cut and carved in any direction without splitting or cracking.

Pestered by pilgrims

Like all 14th-century Christians, you honour saints and believe that their prayers will help you get to heaven. Canterbury Cathedral houses the relics (remains) of famous local saint Thomas Becket. A gold, jewelled casket in the Trinity Chapel holds his body; the Corona (a circular chapel) contains part of his skull.

Every year, thousands of pilgrims flock to Canterbury to see the relics. Their gifts of money help pay for building work – but these visitors cause problems! They need food, drink, lodgings and entertainment. And all too often, they get rowdy.

Who d'you think you are – the Archbishop of Canterbury?

It should be a best-seller!

Canterbury Tales

MANY PILGRIMS treat their journey as a jolly holiday. They ride fine horses, stay in cosy inns and amuse each other with funny stories. Right now, England's top poet, Geoffrey Chaucer, is composing a collection of such stories.

In 1370, Archbishop Sudbury had to run for his life when angry pilgrims attacked him, after he had scolded them for bad behaviour.

Handy hint

Fire has destroyed many churches and cathedrals – including Canterbury. So be careful where pilgrims leave the candles that are symbols of their prayers.

I shall not be moved.

I wonder how fast he can run in those robes.

Royal resting place

KINGS AND PRINCES pay good money to be buried in the cathedral. Best known is Edward the 'Black Prince', son of King Edward III and husband of local heiress Joan, the 'Fair Maid of Kent'. When this famous warrior died in 1376, Henry Yevele (see page 71) designed a magnificent gold and bronze tomb for him.

He never wore shoes like that, you know. Not while I knew him.

Why was Edward called the Black Prince? Some say that it's because he wore black armour or carried a black shield, but nobody knows for sure.

81

Building for the future

Well! You've seen what the future might hold if you choose to be a cathedral builder: long years of study, tough tests of skill, hard work, and heavy responsibilities. Are you still really sure that it's the right career for you? If so, good luck! But, before you start, there's one other problem to consider. Could you really devote your life to work that you'll never see completed? Not sure? Then think about this: if you could travel hundreds of years into the future, you'd find that most of Europe's great cathedrals are still standing, proud and beautiful – and are still loved, admired and used for prayers by millions of people.

After you're gone...

I'd make it taller.

WARTIME TARGET. In the 17th century, the English Parliament's army will smash stained glass at Canterbury.* In the 20th, Canterbury's towers will be bombed.

A NEW MASTER MASON will take over. Will he honour your plans and your vision – or have his own new ideas?

LONG YEARS of wind, rain, frost and snow will shatter the strongest stone. By the 21st century, Canterbury Cathedral will need urgent work to save it from falling down!

They were very strict Christians and believed it was sinful to admire beautiful images.

Avoid being a Medieval Knight!

Introduction

You are a young boy living in England towards the end of the medieval period, around the year 1400. Your home is in a huge castle, where your father works. He helps manage its vast estates and spends most of his days shut away in his chamber, poring over old documents or checking accounts. Now that you're eight years old, your father wants you to start learning to be a castle official like him. He thinks you should be pleased at the prospect of such a steady career. But you are horrified – that is not what you want to do!

You have always dreamed of becoming a soldier, like the knight who owns the castle. He is a famous fighting man and is one of the king's trusted champions. You admire the knight's strength, his skill and his brave deeds in battle. You envy his riches, his shining armour and his wonderful warhorse. He is your hero and you want to follow his example. But how much do you really know about his life? Are you sure you want to be a medieval knight?

Glamorous Knights

To be a Knight:

KNIGHTS are meant to follow rules of good behaviour, called 'chivalry'. They must promise to be:

efore you decide on your future career, check out what you know about knights. They are elite warriors who fight on horseback. They help lead the armies of kings or noble lords. Some are brave and generous, others are cowardly, or cruel. To show respect for their high rank, knights are always called 'Sir'. There have been knights for hundreds of years. They first became important around AD 800.

Gentle

Brave

Generous

Merciful

Pious

Oh, isn't he handsome!

Hands off – he's mine!

...and also courteous, gallant, obedient, patient and persevering!

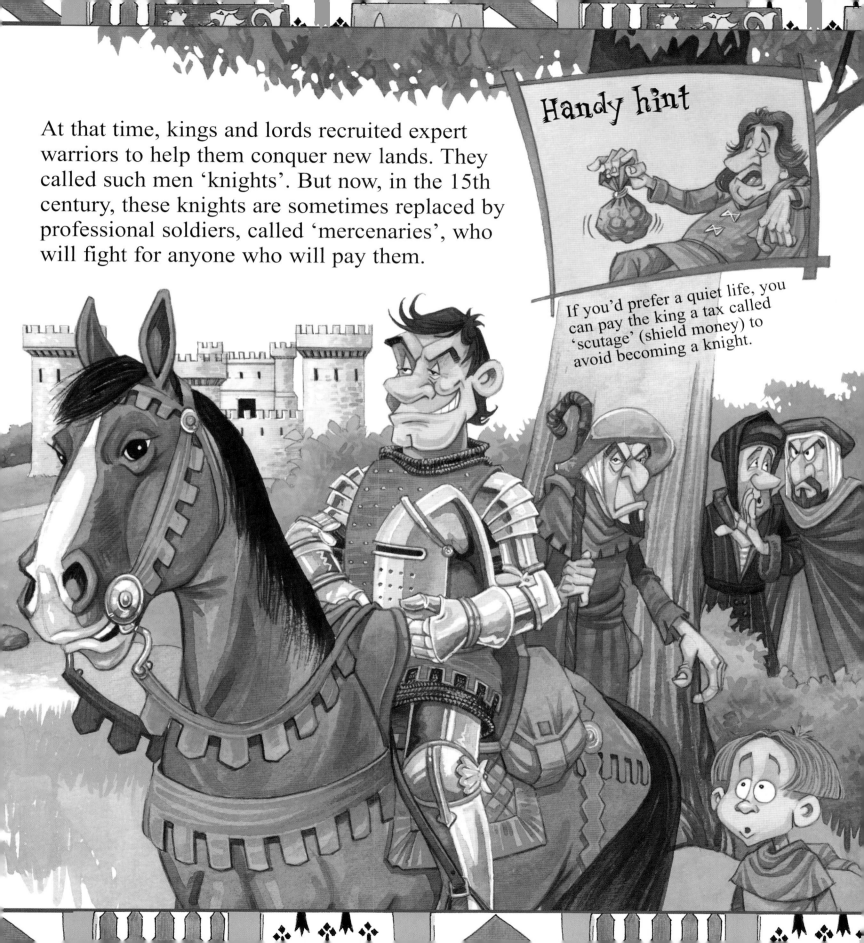

At that time, kings and lords recruited expert warriors to help them conquer new lands. They called such men 'knights'. But now, in the 15th century, these knights are sometimes replaced by professional soldiers, called 'mercenaries', who will fight for anyone who will pay them.

Handy hint

If you'd prefer a quiet life, you can pay the king a tax called 'scutage' (shield money) to avoid becoming a knight.

Do you have a rich, noble family?

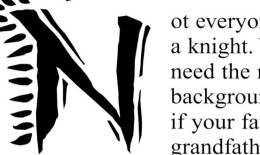

Not everyone can become a knight. You normally need the right family background – it helps if your father and grandfather were knights before you. But men from ordinary families can also be made knights as a reward for bravery in battle. Women cannot become knights, though they often help defend castles from attackers or accompany armies as cooks and nurses. Most knights' families own large estates, given to them long ago by the kings or lords they promised to fight for. In return for this land, knights have many duties, in peacetime as well as in war.

National duties

FIGHTING. You'll have to fight in the king's army and lead your own troop of soldiers in war.

FRIENDSHIP. You'll have to be a good companion to the king and share in all his leisure pursuits.

COUNSELLING. You'll have to offer the king wise advice – even if he doesn't like what you have to say.

Hmm...she doesn't look too bad for a wife.

Handy hint

Your family will choose a wife to help and support you – whether you like her or not!

I'll have my own suit of armour one day!

Local duties

FARMING. You'll have to manage your family's lands and give orders to the peasants working there.

FINANCE. You'll have to collect royal taxes. That will make you very unpopular with everyone!

LEGAL GUARDIAN. You'll have to protect the local peasants at times of conflict as well as settling quarrels between them.

Time to start training

Are you ready to leave your home and family? It takes many years' training to become a knight and most boys start at the age of eight. Your parents will send you to another castle, belonging to a well-respected knight. He'll teach you many new skills, but he almost certainly won't understand how homesick you'll feel. You'll meet several other boys at his castle, all hoping to be knights, like you. The youngest will work as pages (household servants) and grooms (stableboys). The eldest will serve as squires (personal assistants), taking important messages, carrying weapons, leading horses and helping knights to get ready for battle.

Learning to be a Knight

WAITING AT TABLES and serving food will teach you good manners and neat, nimble habits.

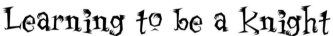

BUILD UP YOUR MUSCLES. Training with heavy wooden swords will make you strong enough to fight with real weapons.

LEARNING TO HUNT with hawks will teach you to observe your surroundings and be a good lookout.

HORSE SENSE. Feeding and grooming large warhorses will teach you how to handle them when it's time to ride off to battle.

C'mon lad. If you want to be a Knight you have to leave home.

TARGET PRACTICE. Riding at a quintain (a target fixed to a swivelling pole with a weight at the other end) will teach you how to fight with a lance (below).

Handy hint

Watch out for bullies! You'll find several bigger boys training at the same castle as you.

Quintain

Lance

Ooof!

91

Loyalty to your lord

Knights are meant to be loyal. They swear oaths (solemn promises) to be faithful to the king and to their lord. The first and most important of these oaths takes place when a squire has completed his training and is ready to become a knight. This usually happens about the age of 21. The evening before the ceremony, he has a bath and puts on clean clothes. Then he goes to the castle chapel and spends the night in prayer. The next morning, he kneels before the king – or his lord – and promises to serve him loyally. The king then dubs (taps) him on the shoulder, saying 'Arise, Sir Knight.'

Arise, Sir Knight.

THE RIGHT ROBES? The king or your lord will give you a uniform, called 'livery', made to his own design. Your squire will help you dress (left).

PICTURE PUZZLE. You will have to learn how to read heraldic designs (right). Each noble family has its own coat of arms, which they'll expect you to recognise.

Handy hint

Be careful if you're chosen to carry a banner into battle. It will make you an easy target for the enemy.

WIN YOUR SPURS! As a new knight, you'll have to prove your courage and skills on the battlefield. Medieval people call this 'winning your spurs'.

Spurs

Only knights fight on horseback and need to wear spurs.

DON'T CHOOSE A LOSER! You'll meet many rival lords (left). Only one can bring you success. Those lords on the wrong 'side' – and the knights serving them – might end up losing their lives!

WANT TO BE PAID TO FIGHT? Then join a band of mercenary soldiers (right). They'll fight for anyone who gives them money.

Life in a castle

Castle conditions

Living in a castle is not always easy, pleasant or comfortable. How could you cope with:

You have spent all your life in other knights' castles. Do you really want one as your own home? Castles are very expensive to build, or dangerously hard work if you want to capture someone else's! Once you have a castle, you must keep it in good repair and pay for soldiers to guard it night and day. Inside, castles are becoming more cosy than they have been for centuries. You'll find private rooms for you and your family, with fireplaces in most rooms and tapestries hanging on the walls. Most castles are still cold and draughty in winter and horribly smelly in the summer – especially when sewage from the garderobes (lavatories) leaks into the castle moat!

freezing-cold battlements;

rowdy soldiers in their quarters;

a flaming-hot kitchen;

a rising drawbridge;

a noisy, fiery forge;

a fast-falling portcullis;

and a dismal dungeon?

Get Kitted out

ompared with ordinary foot soldiers, knights are very fortunate. They have armour to protect them in battle. In the past, this was made of chain mail but it is now usually made of 'plates' – shaped pieces of metal, carefully joined together. This new armour looks very impressive, but it is also extremely expensive. As a new knight, you'll probably have to make do with hand-me-downs from your family.

DRESSED TO KILL. You will need help from a squire to put on your armour, but it only takes about 15 minutes. Be careful to fasten all the separate pieces properly, otherwise the result could be disastrous! First of all, put on a padded tunic which includes chain mail sections (1). Attach a chain mail kilt (2). Put on the plate armour, carefully fastening all the straps (3). Finally, add your helmet and gauntlets (4).

1

2

3

4

Visor to cover face

Breastplate

Chain-mail kilt

Gauntlets (gloves)

Greaves (shin guards)

Alternatively, you could buy second-hand armour, or loot some from a dead knight during battle! Whether it's old or new, all armour clanks, creaks and chafes. It's hot and heavy to wear and can slow you down, trip you up, or get in the way of your weapons. Remember – even the best armour is not guaranteed to save you. In battle, you'll always have to fight for your life!

Handy hint

Don't be old-fashioned! Remember, styles of armour change over the years.

Rivet

Metal ring

MAKING A CHAIN MAIL tunic is extremely time-consuming (above). Thousands of separate rings have to be shaped from metal wire, linked with their neighbours, then held in place by rivets. More modern plate armour is a little quicker to create.

97

Armed and dangerous

I n battle, you will rely on your weapons. You should own five or six different kinds: a mace, a long sword, a short sword, a battle-axe, a lance and maybe a dagger. All are sharp, awkward and heavy – just one sword will weigh over a kilo – and you must be able to handle them well, without injuring yourself. You will have to decide which weapons to use for defending yourself and which for attacking your enemies. Whichever you choose, act quickly, or an enemy soldier will kill you while you're still making up your mind! The latest lethal weapon is a war hammer, designed to kill knights wearing plate armour by dealing them deadly blows. However, you have to be brave enough to get close to your enemy to hit him!

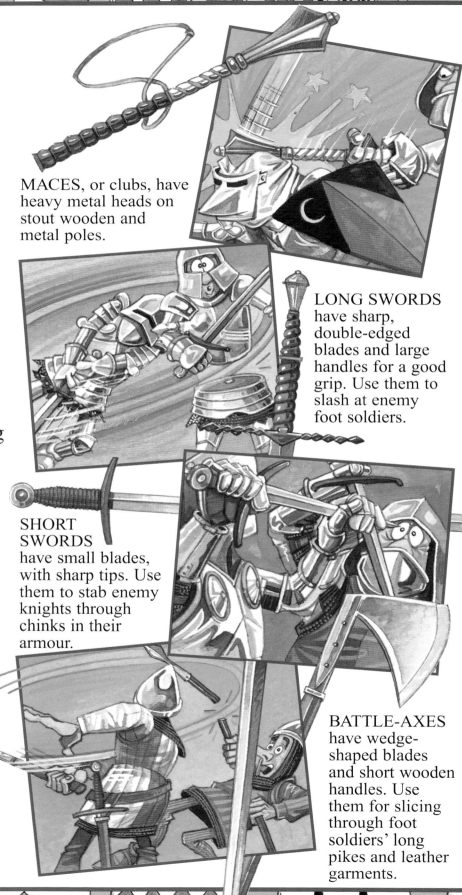

MACES, or clubs, have heavy metal heads on stout wooden and metal poles.

LONG SWORDS have sharp, double-edged blades and large handles for a good grip. Use them to slash at enemy foot soldiers.

SHORT SWORDS have small blades, with sharp tips. Use them to stab enemy knights through chinks in their armour.

BATTLE-AXES have wedge-shaped blades and short wooden handles. Use them for slicing through foot soldiers' long pikes and leather garments.

Coping on Crusade

"Phew – that was close!"

Since 1096, European soldiers, known as 'Crusaders', have been fighting in the Holy Land – the area around the city of Jerusalem. Crusaders hope to win this land from the Muslims who have ruled it since AD 637. More recently, there have been Crusades in north-east Europe to force pagan peoples living there into becoming Christians. Most Crusaders do not return from the Holy Land but die, either on the journey or from sickness, or are killed by Muslim soldiers. These troops fight in a way that you've never seen before, shooting at the marching Crusading armies with bows and arrows before galloping away!

A dangerous journey...

EXPECT TO FEEL SICK as you sail to the Holy Land, especially if this is your first long journey by sea.

TRY NOT TO WORRY about being shipwrecked. Only a few of the Crusaders' ships sink on each voyage!

DON'T GET STUCK in a snowdrift as you cross the mountains. Dig yourself out quickly, or you'll die of cold!

Handy hint

The Holy Land is hot! Copy Muslim soldiers and wear a loose surcoat over your armour. It will help you keep cool!

...to a dangerous place

KEEP FLEAS OUT of your tent in the Holy Land. They carry the germs that cause plague, which can kill you!

STAY AWAY FROM SNAKES! Most are not deadly poisonous, but their bites can be very painful.

DON'T RUN OUT OF WATER in the desert. Always carry plenty with you, or you'll die of thirst!

Surviving a siege

Sieges are sometimes the only way to capture castles or walled cities. You need patience – and huge war machines – to carry out a successful siege. You must organise your army to surround the enemy city or castle and give them orders to stop anyone from entering or leaving. Then you have to wait, until the supplies of food and water run out inside and the inhabitants either starve or surrender. If you are particularly cunning or cruel you might torture enemy captives outside the walls, to warn defenders what will happen if they don't give in.

Germ warfare

SPREAD SICKNESS by polluting enemy water supplies with the rotting corpses of dead animals. Germ-laden dead bodies can also be hurled over enemy walls.

CLEVER 'CAT' (movable shed). This shelters sappers (also known as miners) – soldiers digging tunnels under enemy walls to make them crumble and collapse.

Handy hint

If you want to survive a siege, surrender straight away. If the besiegers manage to break in, you won't live long.

TREBUCHET. When one end is pulled down, the other shoots up and flings rocks high over enemy defences.

Keep up the bombardment, men! Their defences won't hold for much longer.

BRUTAL BATTERING RAM. Made of a huge tree trunk and tipped with iron, a battering ram is strong enough to smash holes in gates and crack stonework.

BIG BELFRY – that's what the soldiers call this tall siege tower. From the top, they can shoot arrows at defenders on the battlements.

MURDEROUS MANGONEL. This giant catapult can hurl huge lumps of rock through the air. Its power comes from ropes twisted tightly, then released.

Bravery in battle

Look out for:

GUNNERS, who try to kill you with shot (stone or metal balls); longbowmen, who try to kill you with sharp, feathered arrows; and crossbowmen, who try to kill you with metal bolts.

Gun (used from c. 1400)

Longbow

Crossbow

In battle, you'll face many different types of fighters, as well as other knights. Most enemy troops ranged against you will be foot soldiers. They make up the majority of most medieval armies and are recruited from rough, tough peasants. Many such soldiers are angry at being ordered away from their fields by their king or lord.

They want to win battles quickly and then go home, which can make them vicious enemies! Compared with knights, most foot soldiers are only part-time fighters, but this does not make them any less dangerous. They are armed with various types of deadly weapons, including pikes, pitchforks and wooden clubs. Their bows shoot bolts and arrows that fall like 'killer rain' on the enemy – including you!

Handy hint

Bind up wounds with egg-soaked bandages and stop bleeding by cauterising wounds with a red-hot iron.

Don't fall off your horse!

A knight's most important possessions are his warhorses. Fierce stallions, called 'destriers' and 'coursers', are specially bred for battle. Warhorses must be extremely strong, to carry knights with their weapons and armour. By nature they are aggressive and they are also trained to bite and kick. A good warhorse is very expensive and you'll need at least two! Knights also need pack-horses to carry baggage, and riding horses for squires and grooms.

IN BATTLE, you line up alongside other knights, holding your lance 'couched' (braced) against your side. When you dig your spurs into his side, your horse will charge towards the enemy!

Beware!

STAY AWAY FROM STAKES! Half buried, pointing upwards, these sharp wooden poles kill many horses and riders.

CHAAARGE!

Caltrops

BEWARE OF BOGS! Don't let damp, soggy ground trap you and your horse and sink your chance of victory.

PREPARE FOR PITS! Your enemies will dig pits, then cover them with leaves or grass ready for you to fall into.

BE CAREFUL OF CALTROPS! These iron spikes, scattered on the ground, cruelly dig into horses' hooves.

107

So many ways to die...

From the start of your training as a knight, your life will be at risk. It's hard to know for sure, but most fighting men die before they are 50 years old. All knights hope to be remembered after they die. Many pay artists to create lifelike portraits of them, to be displayed in the church where they will be buried. They pay priests to say prayers and give money to charity so that poor people will remember them gratefully. If you plan on becoming a knight, do as others do and order your tomb straight away!

Try not to...

DIE IN BATTLE, in pain and surrounded by the enemy.

DIE FROM INFECTED WOUNDS, a miserable, lingering death.

DIE FROM DYSENTERY, an awful sickness.

DIE IN PRISON, locked in chains, then abandoned.

and try to...

DIE FROM HEATSTROKE, half cooked inside your armour.

DIE FROM FROSTBITE, shivering and chilled to the bone.

BE SEVERELY INJURED and unable to work for the rest of your life.

DIE PEACEFULLY IN YOUR BED. That is actually how many retired knights end their days!

Avoid being in a Medieval Dungeon!

Introduction

t is the end of the 15th century in medieval England. You are a tough, battle-scarred soldier who has just returned home after fighting wars in faraway countries. You are happy to have survived, even though your shoulder has been badly wounded and your arm is broken.

You won't be much use as a fighter from now on, but your injuries are healing and you start to feel better. You're also feeling poor! You have spent all your soldier's wages and have nothing to live on. You need to find a job, so you decide to go to the nearest castle, to see what work is available there. You're in luck! The castle needs someone to help run its prison, and the captain of the guard asks if you would like the job. Think carefully! Do you really want to work in a medieval gaol?

A career change

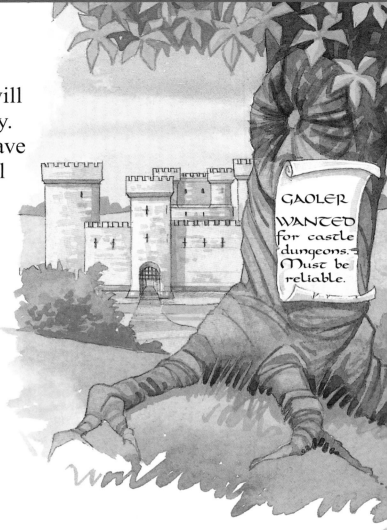

If you become a castle gaoler you will have to work hard and learn quickly. The job is not well paid, but you have power over your prisoners. You will find many ways of making extra money, by demanding bribes and charging fees. There is a good chance of promotion. Experienced prison warders and 'turnkeys' (security guards) are in demand – most castles, cities and towns have at least one gaol. All this means that there are plenty of other people who would like the job.

GAOLER WANTED for castle dungeons. Must be reliable.

Applicants for the job:

AN OLD SERVANT. He knows the castle well and has worked here since he was a boy.

A CRUSADER. Back home after fighting wars in the Middle East, he needs a new job.

A PRIEST. Clever and cunning, he's on the lookout for people who break Church laws.

A MONK. He's in charge of the punishment cell at the local monastery.

A NIGHT-WATCHMAN. He guards the castle gates and is looking for promotion.

I'd steer clear of that place if I were you. Some of those prisoners are a nasty lot!

Handy hint
Women need not apply! Only men can be gaolers in the Middle Ages.

AN IRON-WORKER. He's made all the metal bars that stop prisoners escaping.

THE LOCAL CONSTABLE. He works for the sheriff and arrests people who break the law.

A LOCAL TOWNSMAN. He hopes to make money from working at the gaol.

A TRUSTED OFFICIAL. Elegant and polite, he would be good at dealing with captive nobles and royalty.

A THUG. He will frighten the prisoners but they'll probably outwit him.

113

Who will you work for?

Like all medieval gaolers, you will not have special training. If you get the job it will be because the person who owns the prison thinks you can be trusted. It is most likely that your employer will be the king. It's his duty to maintain law and order and to protect his kingdom from traitors, rebels and foreign enemies. Most prisons in London belong to him, plus the shire (county) gaols and dungeons in all the royal castles. But many other powerful people have their own private prisons too.

Possible employers

LORDS AND LADIES rule the land around their castles and have their own private prisons. They can punish minor crimes, such as trespass, slander and non-payment of rent.

Lady   *Lord*   *Commander*

ARMY COMMANDERS imprison enemy captives and demand a ransom to set them free.

TOWN COUNCILLORS are in charge of town prisons and are keen to punish crimes by merchants, such as fraud and theft.

Councillor

BISHOPS can imprison people who break the Church's religious laws. The bishops often get involved in quarrels over Church land and property.

Bishop

ABBOTS AND ABBESSES are in charge of religious communities. If monks and nuns break the rules, they are locked in a punishment cell.

Religious investigator

Abbot

RELIGIOUS INVESTIGATORS. Their mission is to get rid of heresy (unlawful beliefs) by torturing confessions out of suspects.

SHERIFFS act as the king's deputy in each shire. Criminals are held in a royal prison until the king's judges hold a trial.

Sheriff

114

IN MEDIEVAL ENGLAND the king's word is law! The most important royal court is called the 'King's Bench'. It gets its name from the seat used by top royal judges, who try suspects accused of serious crimes. Sometimes the king himself sits in the court. Other judges normally visit gaols once or twice a year. They hear the evidence against prisoners accused of less serious crimes and decide whether they are innocent or guilty.

Types of prisons

Once you start work, you will soon discover that prisons are not all the same. In castles, prison cells are often built above the main gates in the outer walls. This way, dangerous prisoners cannot get too close to the castle keep. Other castle prisons are hidden deep below ground or in high towers. Sometimes cells are just metal cages hung outside the castle. King Edward I of England kept the wife of a Scottish noble in a cage like this for over a year! City prisons are often built in draughty vaults below the chambers where councillors meet. Empty buildings are sometimes turned into prisons. In Southwark, south of London, the busiest prison is a converted inn called the White Swan.

Oubliette

AN OUBLIETTE (left) is a narrow, tube-shaped prison, without windows. The only way in is through a trapdoor at the top. Prisoners are lowered down on a rope and left to rot! Sometimes water seeps in from the bottom and they drown.

YOU MIGHT have to shut prisoners in a 'little ease' – a tiny room, hollowed out of castle walls (right). Some of these cramped chambers are so small that prisoners cannot lie down, sit comfortably or even turn around.

Bottle dungeon

Handy hint

Once you have gained experience, give advice to builders and architects. They might pay you for tips on how to make a prison really secure.

Bottle dungeons (above left) are deep underground prisons. Tall stone towers (right) keep prisoners high in the air. Both are designed to prevent escapes and hide prisoners away from friends who might help them.

What have I done to deserve this?

SOME CASTLES have private rooms where rich or noble prisoners are locked up in nice surroundings. They may even be allowed to stroll in the castle's gardens (above).

Little ease

Castle life

L ife in a medieval castle is extremely busy. It is like a whole village community inside strong stone walls. There is never a quiet moment, from sunrise to after dark. There are soldiers shouting, blacksmiths hammering, horses whinnying, pigs grunting, babies crying, women chattering, workmen grumbling, messengers cursing and, above it all, the lord of the castle barking out commands. Heavy farm carts, full of vital supplies, rumble over the stone courtyard. Labourers grunt and sweat as they unload sacks of grain. It's no wonder you can't sleep in your off-duty hours!

119

Criminals, traitors and outlaws

As a gaoler, you'll have to deal with people accused of many different crimes. There are highway robbers, counterfeiters, traitors and other 'enemies of the state'. All will have been arrested on suspicion and put in prison to wait for months or years for judges to arrive. Take care! Many prisoners will be angry, violent or despairing and some of them are dangerous. All will be frightened that one day soon, they might die. Death is the punishment for serious crimes such as murder, treason, forgery or robbery with violence.

Dead scared

All these prisoners (right) face the death penalty if they are found guilty. People who commit less serious crimes are fined, flogged or left to rot in prison for a while.

Pirate   *Murderer*   *Burglar*

Traitor or rebel   Plotter   Outlaw   Counterfeiter   Corrupt official

Bad company

You will probably believe that most of your prisoners are a bad lot, even though many of them have not committed a crime. Some are in prison because they have powerful enemies. People are also imprisoned because they are thought to be witches or have strange beliefs. Some prisoners will be there simply through bad luck. Other prisoners are certainly guilty, but hardship and poverty might have forced them into stealing or breaking the law. However, like most medieval people, you think that people should accept their fate and have no excuse to break the law.

SHEEP-STEALING. A nice fat sheep makes a tempting target for hungry thieves. It can feed a poor family for at least a week.

STOP, THIEF!

LIFE IS HORRIBLE for ordinary people in the Middle Ages. Most are poor and many are not free to leave their lord's lands. They are often cold, tired and hungry. It is not surprising that some become criminals.

THE CATHOLIC CHURCH is powerful throughout Europe. Church leaders believe that only they know the truth about God. Anyone with different beliefs is guilty of heresy, which is a deadly sin.

Handy hint

See what advice you can get from any 'witches' in your prison. Such people often know about healing herbs, poisons and so-called 'magic spells'.

HOME LIFE can be stressful. Many people have arranged marriages. Whatever their feelings, husbands and wives have to stay together, or starve. There is no state welfare system, so poverty drives people to commit crime.

SOLDIERS CAPTURED IN BATTLE face a gloomy future. They will be kept in prison until their families pay a ransom to set them free. If they cannot afford to do this, then the soldiers may be killed.

Only 126 miles to go.

Innocent victims

I t is hard to dislike all your prisoners – some are innocent victims with heartbreaking stories. Often these people have found themselves behind bars because somebody powerful wants them out of the way. Maybe they have angered the royal family or know embarrassing secrets. Perhaps they have rival claims to inherit a rich estate or even the throne! Many such prisoners are women and children. The young English princes, Edward, aged 12, and Richard, aged 9 (right), were locked in the Tower of London by their uncle, King Richard III, in 1483. He then had them murdered so they could not grow up and take over his throne.

SHIPWRECKED SAILORS are arrested and locked up until they can prove who they are.

FRIENDS who have quarrelled with someone powerful may be carried off to gaol.

WOMEN WHO REJECT royal offers of love or marriage might be put in prison until they change their minds.

FOREIGN AMBASSADORS are sent to prison when wars begin. They were friends before, but have suddenly become enemies.

ROYAL WIVES who fail to give birth to a son might be shut away because they are useless!

PEOPLE WITH MENTAL ILLNESSES are locked up, to keep them safe, but others cruelly come to laugh at them.

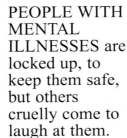

Handy hint
Invite the public to visit your prison. They'll pay you to let them gawp at pretty princesses, wounded warriors or people who are mentally ill.
Wh...what was that noise?

Dealing with prisoners

Medieval prisons are terrible places. Most prisoners will beg you to set them free or at least move them out of the damp, dark, crowded cells. You must be hardhearted. If you let anyone escape, you'll lose your job, be beaten, or even be executed!

I'll give you anything you want if I get out of here, just for a piece of that pie!

CONDITIONS INSIDE gaols are disgusting. But most gaolers do not care! If prisoners cannot arrange for someone to bring them food, candles and bedding, they will suffer terribly.

dark...

and crowded!

Cells are slimy...

damp...

Prisoners will plead for food, water and other basic comforts, such as straw to sleep on or the chance to warm themselves by a fire in winter. Nothing – no food, water or bedding – is supplied by the owner of the gaol. Prisoners' friends and families must provide these items. You can offer to get supplies, if the prisoners can pay you!

Handy hint

Don't keep a dog or a cat – they'll chase the rats and mice away! You want your prison to be as nasty as possible!

YOU CAN MAKE extra money by demanding a fee from the friends, business colleagues and lawyers who visit prisoners (left).

YOU MIGHT LET starving prisoners beg for food through the bars of their cells (right). With luck, passers-by will take pity on them.

No beds

No toilets

Rats, lice and fleas

You need a strong stomach and a strong mind to cope with prison conditions. Most cells are infested with insects and most prisoners are covered with lice or hopping with fleas. Rats, lizards, beetles and cockroaches scurry across the damp, dirty floors. As well as scaring sensitive prisoners, these creatures can carry serious diseases. The worst are typhus fever and plague, also known as the Black Death! Many prisoners die from disease before they ever come to trial. Prisons are also very smelly. Inside, they reek of stale blood, sweat and sewage. Outside most prison walls, you can't escape the smell of stagnant moats, blocked drains, privies and stables.

RAIN, SNOW and cold, damp air blow through the prison bars and chill everyone locked up inside. Many prisoners die from hypothermia (extremely low body temperature).

FLEAS carry plague germs in their saliva. Lice carry the germs that cause typhus fever. If the bugs bite you, you will catch these diseases.

RATS also carry plague, a terrible illness. Victims get huge boils in their groins and armpits, bleed from the mouth (and elsewhere), run a high temperature, become delirious and die.

DIRTY, SMELLY WATER carries germs and tiny microorganisms that cause vomiting and diarrhoea. Prisoners have to risk drinking it – or die of thirst.

Handy hint

Copy the judges who hold trials in prisons. They carry posies of herbs and flowers because they believe the sweet smell will kill diseases carried in foul air.

The soft option

Sometimes it's a good idea to treat prisoners kindly, especially those who might be in a position to help you if they're set free. Even the most powerful men and women will be grateful if you make their stay in prison as comfortable as possible. Let them bring their own books, furniture, musical instruments, servants and children. Let them continue to have a hobby or work. Top tailors imprisoned in London bring their sewing kits with them so that they can still make clothes for customers. This way they earn money to pay for luxuries while behind bars.

EVEN THE MOST COMFORTABLE PRISONS can be dangerous places. Poison or 'accidents' are the most usual methods of quietly getting rid of important prisoners. The Duke of Clarence was found drowned in a cask of wine at the Tower of London, in 1478!

Is there anything I can do for you, m'lady?

EXERCISE stops prisoners growing restless and dangerous. The guards at Fleet prison, in London, let rich prisoners play skittles all day long.

WIVES AND MOTHERS often ask to bring food in for their families. Let them do this, but search the meals for hidden weapons or tools.

FRIARS need your permission to preach and say prayers in prison. Welcome them! Their holy words might help your sinful soul.

What a creep!

Handy hint

There will be some visitors your prisoners don't want to see, such as enemies who could taunt or bully them. Offer to keep them out – for a fee!

LOOK FORWARD to a better job! You may get this as a reward from powerful people you have helped in gaol.

YOU CAN EXPECT gifts and bribes in return for treating prisoners kindly. Don't be too greedy!

BE POLITE to important people, even if they are prisoners. They might be powerful again one day.

131

No escape!

There are plenty of ways to ensure your prisoners are secure. To begin with, you'll rely on heavy wooden doors with strong locks and bolts, and iron bars across all the windows. You will probably choose to keep the most dangerous or high-risk prisoners fastened to cell walls, using handcuffs and leg-fetters that are attached to heavy iron chains. If you are cruel, you can arrange for these to be fixed so the prisoner can't move or can't touch the floor.

To force prisoners to confess to crimes, gaolers use torture. The most common tortures are: the red-hot iron, which burns; the rack, which stretches prisoners and destroys their joints; the boot, which crushes prisoners' legs; and thumbscrews, which squeeze fingers until the fingernails fall off.

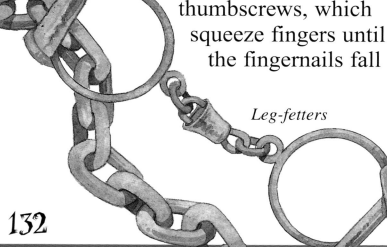

Leg-fetters

No! Not the red-hot iron!

132

This might sting just a little bit...

Handy hint

Fancy new locks are being invented all the time. Don't be too keen to use them! You might lock yourself in — and no-one would know how to set you free!

Pillory

Stocks

Other punishments

THIEVES can be locked in a pillory (above left), where their heads and hands are trapped while the public throws rubbish at them. Or you could shut them in the stocks (above) so the people they've cheated can pelt them with mud and rotten food.

IF A WOMAN is known to be a gossip and scold, then tie her to a ducking stool (left) and dip her in the river. That will teach her to hold her tongue!

Ducking stool

133

Freedom or death

Very few prisoners manage to escape from gaol or can pay the vast sums of ransom money to be set free. Those with powerful friends can expect to be released if a new king comes to the throne or when new politicians win power. Most prisoners find that death is the only way out of gaol. They die in prison from cold, hunger, torture or disease – or they are executed. Noble men and women are beheaded, which is quick and almost painless. Ordinary criminals are condemned to be hanged – a slow, very painful way to die.

Can't we talk about this...?

SOME PRISONERS get out of gaol more peacefully. They might be found not guilty and set free. They might be forgiven their crimes and receive a royal pardon. They might escape in disguise. Or they might die and be free from suffering at last.

Not guilty

Death

Escape in disguise

A pardon

Handy hint

Retire as soon as you can! As a gaoler, you'll have made many enemies. Some people will look for revenge – you don't want to end up in gaol yourself!

SAVED BY A SONG! King Richard the Lionheart of England (ruled 1189-1199) was captured by enemies while returning from a war. No-one knew where he was being held. Legend tells that his minstrel travelled Europe, singing Richard's favourite song while looking for him. When the king sang back, the minstrel knew he had found him!

135

Glossary

Abbess The leader of a religious community of nuns.

Abbot The leader of a religious community of monks.

Almonry An office where charity was given to the poor.

Ambassador A senior government official sent to represent his king and country overseas.

Anointed king A king who has been crowned in a ceremony which includes blessing with sacred oil.

Apprentice A young person who learns a trade by working for a master, usually without pay. Medieval apprentices usually lived in the master's house.

Arch A curved structure that spans an opening and supports the weight of the structure above it.

Archbishop A top-ranking bishop with authority over other bishops.

Armoury A store for armour and weapons.

Bailiff The official in charge of farming on a lord's estate.

Banner A flag carried by a knight who commanded other knights.

Barracks Soldiers' living quarters.

Bishop A senior churchman with authority over ordinary priests.

Bolt A short arrow, fired by a crossbow.

Brewhouse A place for making ale. Ale was safer to drink than untreated water.

Bribe A payment made in return for a special favour.

Budget The amount of money available to spend on a project.

Buttery The place where wine and beer were kept, in 'butts' (barrels).

Buttress A strong, heavy prop built against a wall to prevent it from leaning.

Byzantine Empire A Christian empire formed from the eastern part of the old Roman Empire. In the late 11th century it covered most of the Balkans, the Greek islands, Cyprus and Turkey. Its capital was Constantinople (now Istanbul).

Caliph The leader of the Sunni (majority) branch of the faith of Islam.

Caltrops Sharp metal spikes, scattered in front of horses to wound them and stop them advancing.

Cannibalism The act of eating another human being.

Capital A block at the top of a pillar, carved in a decorative shape.

Cathedral A Christian church that is the headquarters of a bishop.

Cauterise To burn body tissue in order to seal it and stop bleeding.

Chain mail Armour made of hundreds of small metal rings, interlinked and fastened together.

Chamberlain The official in charge of a lord's household arrangements.

Chandlery A place for making candles.

Chapel A smaller place of worship within a church or other building.

Chivalry The rules of good behaviour that all knights were supposed to follow.

Cloister A courtyard with a covered walkway around the edge.

Coat of arms A badge worn by a knight to show which noble family he belonged to.

Column A cylindrical pillar.

Constable The commander of a castle.

Counterfeiter A maker of fake coins.

Courteous Polite and considerate.

Crusades Wars fought from the 11th to the 16th centuries by European Christians to recapture the Holy Land from the Muslims. There were also Crusades against pagans (non-Christians) in northern Europe, against rebel Christians in France and Germany, and against Muslims in Spain.

Damsel A young lady, or a lady-in-waiting.

Dispensary A place where medicines were made.

Distaff A tool for spinning wool to make thread.

Dub To tap on the shoulder with a sword. It is part of the ceremony of becoming a knight.

Dysentery An infectious disease that causes terrible sickness and diarrhoea. It is often fatal if modern medicines are not available.

Elite Best, or highest-ranking.

Estate The land belonging to a castle.

Farrier An officer who looked after horses.

Fetters Curved iron bars that could be locked around prisoners' legs.

Flying buttress A buttress that is built some distance away from a wall, and connected to it by half-arches.

Foundation The lowest part of a building, below ground, which supports the weight of the whole building.

Fraud Cheating.

Friar A priest who lived close to poor and needy people in medieval communities.

Frieze A band of carved decoration along the surface of a wall.

Gaol Another word for prison; sometimes spelled 'jail'.

Garderobe A lavatory. The word means 'clothes guard' – medieval people believed that the smell from lavatories kept away insects that ate woollen cloth.

Gluttony Too great a liking for food.

Great Chamber The second most important room in the keep, after the Great Hall. It was a more private living space for the lord and his family.

Great Hall The main room of a keep. Used for official business such as trying criminals and receiving visitors, it was also a communal dining room and sleeping quarters.

Guild A society or brotherhood for members of a particular trade or profession. It provides help for members, and may try to prevent non-members from following the trade.

Heraldic Belonging to heraldry – the study of coats of arms.

Heresy Any religious belief that goes against the teaching of the Church.

Hermit A person who lives apart from the rest of society, usually in a wild, lonely place, to devote himself to God.

Holy Land The land around the holy city of Jerusalem in the Middle East.

Journeyman A worker who has finished his apprenticeship but has not yet qualified as a master. He is paid by the day, and the name comes from the French word *journée*, meaning 'a day's work'.

Keep A modern name for the strong central tower of a castle; an older name for it is **donjon**.

Knight A mounted warrior who fought for his lord and was given an estate in return.

Lance A long spear, used on horseback.

Livery A uniform worn by soldiers fighting in the same knight's army.

Mace A war club, usually with a spiked metal head.

Magna Carta A legal agreement made in June 1215 between King John of England and his barons (lords). It removed some power from the king and gave some rights to the people. The name means 'Great Charter'.

Man-at-arms A highly trained soldier without the status of a knight.

Marshal The official in charge of stables, hunting and military forces.

Mason A worker who builds in stone.

Master A worker who has passed an examination to prove that he is skilled in his trade. He is allowed to employ other workers and to train apprentices.

Master mason A mason who has qualified as a master; also, the head mason on a building project.

Masterpiece A test-piece made by a worker as part of the examination to become a master.

Medieval Belonging to the Middle Ages (the years from around AD 1000 to AD 1500).

Mêlée A fighting contest between groups of knights. A victor kept his opponent's horse – a valuable prize.

Mercenary A soldier who fights for pay, not out of loyalty to his country or ruler.

Minstrel A professional musician or entertainer.

Moat A defensive ditch, usually filled with water.

Molten Melted by heating to a very high temperature.

Monastery The home of a community of monks.

Multicultural Involving the cultures of several different nations.

Niche A shallow opening in a wall, usually to hold a statue.

Nomads People without a settled home, who move from place to place to live.

Outlaw A criminal who is not protected by the law and may be killed on sight.

Page A boy of knightly family sent from home to train for knighthood.

Pallet A thin mattress stuffed with straw.

Peasant A poor farmer who makes a living from the land.

Persevering Refusing to give in when faced with danger or difficulty.

Pike A long spear used by foot soldiers.

Pilgrim A person who makes a long journey to worship at a holy place.

Pillar A tall, narrow support for a roof or a wall.

Pinnacle A tall, narrow ornament, often on the top of a buttress.

Pious Devoted to religion.

Pitchfork A huge, two-pronged fork, normally used as a farming tool.

Plague A deadly disease caused by bacteria (germs) that were passed to humans by fleas that lived on rats.

Plate armour Armour made from thin sheets of metal, carefully shaped and fitted together.

Pope The leader of the Roman Catholic branch of the Christian Church.

Portcullis A metal gate that dropped down to bar the entrance to a castle.

Pulpit The platform on which a priest stands to lead prayers or give a sermon.

Quintain A swivelling target used to practise fighting with a lance.

Rafter A sloping piece of wood which is part of the structure of a roof.

Ransom Money paid for the release of a prisoner. Holding important prisoners to ransom was considered a normal part of medieval warfare.

Reeve An official elected annually by estate workers to represent their interests with the bailiff and the courts.

Relic A part of a saint's body, or an article that belonged to a saint.

Rib A narrow band of stone which helps to strengthen a vault.

Rushes Marsh plants whose long, stiff, grasslike leaves were used as disposable floor coverings.

Scaling ladder A long ladder used by attackers to climb a wall.

Scold The medieval word for a woman who was always telling off other people or gossiping.

Scribe A person who writes or copies official documents.

Scutage A tax paid by men from rich or noble families who did not want to become knights.

Sea legs The ability to keep your balance and avoid seasickness on board ship.

Sermon A speech made by a priest, teaching people how they should behave.

Sheriff An officer who enforced the law in a county.

Shrine A place where a saint is commemorated, especially a place that has relics of the saint.

Slander Telling lies about someone.

Sloth The sin of laziness.

Smithy A blacksmith's workshop.

Spurs Sharp spikes fixed to the heel-pieces of a knight's footwear. They were pressed into a horse's side to make it run more quickly.

Squire A youth in the second stage of knightly training, acting as a servant to a knight.

Stocks A low wooden frame with holes for a criminal's feet. Offenders were locked in the stocks as a punishment.

Surcoat A long, loose tunic made of lightweight fabric, worn over a suit of armour.

Template A pattern of wood or metal which is used as a guide for shaping something that needs to be made.

Tenant A person who rents land and property from the person who owns it.

Tournament A sporting contest that included various types of mock combat.

Traitor A person who betrays their country or their ruler.

Trencher A slice of stale bread used as a plate; later, a wooden plate.

Trespass To enter someone's private property without permission.

Truckle bed A low bed on wheels, used by a servant. It was put away beneath the master's or mistress's bed.

Vault A roof with an arched shape, which is much stronger than a flat or sloping roof; also a cellar or underground room.

Villein A peasant entirely subject to his lord, not owning the land he lived on and not allowed to leave it.

Index